Henry Dunckley

Richard Cobden And the Jubilee of Free Trade

Henry Dunckley

Richard Cobden And the Jubilee of Free Trade

ISBN/EAN: 9783744723763

Printed in Europe, USA, Canada, Australia, Japan

Cover: Foto ©ninafisch / pixelio.de

More available books at **www.hansebooks.com**

RICHARD COBDEN AND THE JUBILEE OF FREE TRADE

By HENRY DUNCKLEY, D.C.L.; M. PAUL LEROY-BEAULIEU ; THEODOR BARTII ; THE RIGHT HON. LEONARD COURTNEY, M.P., AND THE RIGHT HON. CHARLES PEL- HAM VILLIERS, M.P.

WITH INTRODUCTION
By RICHARD GOWING

LONDON: T. FISHER UNWIN
PATERNOSTER SQUARE, 1896

CONTENTS

INTRODUCTION

RICHARD COBDEN lived to see less than twenty years of the half century which has brought us to the Jubilee of the Repeal of the Corn Laws. In his time neither the economic doctrine nor the political policy of Free Trade was seriously challenged after the triumphant return of the Free Trade Parliament of 1852. The Anti-Corn Law League had been revived—in anticipation of Lord Derby's Protectionist appeal to the country—at a meeting at Manchester on the 2d of March, when Mr Cobden declared 'We are going

A

to make an effort to put an end for ever
to this controversy of Free Trade;' and
Mr John Bright said, 'I have not the
shadow of a doubt that, if the question be
fairly put to the constituencies, a large
majority will, in 1852, ratify, confirm and
seal for ever the policy which was adopted
in 1846.' The policy was in due time, in
accordance with Mr Bright's forecast, ratified,
confirmed and sealed by the constituencies,
probably 'for ever;' and from that time forth
Mr Cobden was never confronted by anything in the shape of substantial reaction.
When the Cobden Club was founded, some
months after the great Free Trader's death,
in 1866, the commemorative element in the
club was more conspicuous than the fighting
element. The first hundred gentlemen who
put down their names as concurring in Mr
Thomas Bayley Potter's proposal did so

for the purpose of establishing 'a club on the Fox Club plan, to be associated with the name of Cobden in commemoration of his honest principles, pure life and noble achievements.' But the Cobden Club has covered very much larger ground than the Fox Club—which meets at stated intervals, at, perhaps, the best possible of dinners, and drinks to the pious memory of Charles James Fox. The club which bears the name of the great apostle of Free Trade carries on perpetually a voluminous correspondence with Free Traders and students of the fiscal problems of the time in every part of the world; it brings the Free Traders of the two hemispheres into frequent direct communication; it gathers and stores up and disseminates facts and statistics, collects fresh matter from all sources, and informs and guides public opinion on a question peculiarly apt to be confused by false issue and plausible fallacies. In Mr Gladstone's speech in the chair at the first of the club's dinners, on the 21st of July 1866, there was not one word to indicate to future students of the record that any controversy existed at that time in this country on the question of Free Trade.

'It will,' he said, 'be the general—I would venture to say, the unanimous—sentiment of your countrymen that you have done well to found an institution in connection with his name;' and one of the distinguished chairman's finest points was that in which he gave expression to a feeling which he seemed to regard as one upon which there was no risk of dispute. 'Mr Cobden,' he averred, 'perceived, and not only perceived himself but taught us to perceive, the true moral meaning of trade between nation and nation. He showed that trade was not only a law of wealth and prosperity, but a law of friendship, a law of kindness among all nations; that every single transaction, of which thousands upon thousands are at this moment going on between this country and any other, such as France, was a transaction forming, as it were, one single thread in a web of concord woven between people and people. This,' added Mr Gladstone, 'is one of the ideas now made familiar to us; but permit me to remind you that· this is a modern idea.' The orator spoke as one conscious of addressing himself to something like a universal conviction in the land. Yet this sentiment regarding trade is not quite in tune with the sentiments with which we are familiar to-day — on such a text for example, as 'Made in Germany'—and not one of these

little extracts from Mr Gladstone's first
Cobden Club speech can be said to
correspond in spirit with what may be
called the comment of the enemy, in
the Press and elsewhere, on the speeches
and proceedings of the Cobden Club
Corn Law Repeal Jubilee Dinner of
1896.

It was only in the second division of the
half century that the old issues began to
be raised afresh. But they were absolutely
nothing more than the old issues on which,
in the main, conviction had been brought
home to the minds of men during Cobden's
career. About the beginning of the seventies,
a section of politicians sought to open up a
controversy on the basis of what was called
Reciprocity, with the air of men who had
made a discovery in economics. So short
is the popular memory that—though sound

economists like the late Sir Louis Mallet
had no difficulty in showing clearly enough,
to all who gave any heed, that Free Imports
are a great boon in themselves and far too
valuable to be bartered away in the purchase (if such a thing were practicable) of
the reduction or discontinuance of import
duties in other countries—the discussion on
Reciprocity ran a good many years before it
occurred to anybody to remind the disputants
that Sir Robert Peel had dealt with and
disposed of the argument of Reciprocity in
1846. It may be fairly said that no attempt
worthy of mention was made at the time to
answer Sir Robert Peel on that point. But
the speeches passed out of sight until they
were revived, first, in extracts by the Cobden Club, at the suggestion of Mr I. S.
Leadam, some seven or eight years ago; and
now, in the year of the jubilee, with such

overwhelming force and effect by Mr Villiers, in his reply to the Cobden Club commemoration address, for which a place has been found in this volume.

The country generally paid very little attention, fifty years ago, to those whom Sir Robert Peel challenged in debate on Reciprocity, because the operation of the Corn Laws, and the absolute necessity for their repeal, and the manifest advantages which followed, carried practical conviction to the public mind that the principle involved in the repeal of the Corn Laws was sound, and obviously as salutary with regard to other commodities as with respect to corn.

'Fair Trade' was, of course, only a new name for Reciprocity, adopted as a more taking catch-phrase. In the platform advocacy of the Fair Traders, and in the enormous

mass of pamphlets and leaflets which have
been issued during all these years, no definite
notice has ever been taken of Sir Robert
Peel's unanswerable exposition of the logic
of the position against the Reciprocity policy.
Reciprocity and Fair Trade do not need
much examination before it becomes perfectly
evident that their logical meaning is Protection. It has been the common habit of the
champions of these forms of antagonism to
Free Trade to aver that they are Free
Traders, but only on condition that it is
'Free Trade all round.' This is quite the
same thing as an avowal of the creed of
Protection. The Free Trader is a man who
understands and believes in the beneficence
of Free Imports. Indeed, Free Trade can
have no other meaning, in relation to international commerce, than Free Imports. The
man who does not understand that Free Im-

ports is a saving principle in civilisation has never really understood the question; and when the late Lord Beaconsfield and the Marquis of Salisbury have complained that our Free Trade policy has been in some degree a failure because other countries have not followed our example, and when they have deplored the fact that we have no duties to barter away against tariffs abroad, we know that the Earl of Beaconsfield and Lord Salisbury have never realised the salutary and beneficent principle involved in Free Imports. They have never been Free Traders.

So we have had, since the Repeal of the Corn Laws, roughly speaking, a quarter of a century of comparative Free Trade conviction in the country and a quarter of a century of renewal, in some degree, of the old controversy, in practically the old forms under new names and fresh disguises ; and so it has happened that the Cobden Club gradually found itself in some measure committed to the renewal of the conflict in which Richard Cobden was engaged from the beginning until the election of the Free Trade Parliament of 1852. No doubt the founders of the club realised that much of the work to which Cobden devoted his life, political and economic, was incomplete, and would need watchful championship, and they officially set down their object to be that of 'encouraging the growth and diffusion of those economical and political principles with which Mr Cobden's name is associated.' But at that time the economic disciples of Mr Cobden looked abroad more than at home for the growth and diffusion of the economical principle. Cobden was the 'international man,' and the club was international in spirit and purpose,

on the basis of 'Free Trade, Peace, Good-
will among Nations,' the motto formulated
for the club by Mr Goldwin Smith. There
has never been any club in this country whose
rolls have been enriched with so many names
of eminent men abroad—economists, statesmen
and others—and the club has helped to keep
green in all the lands the memory of Mr
Cobden's unique and remarkable pilgrimages
among the nations. The national jealousy
of this country, which has been constantly
fomented abroad by the apostles of Protection, has in some degree prevented the club
from disseminating Free Trade fact and
argument by the distribution of publications
among the people in foreign countries; but
there are other, though more indirect, ways
—through the club's association with the
apostles of Free Trade in nearly every country
—of keeping the lamp burning which was

set alight by Cobden on his Free Trade travels.

It was in the early autumn of last year, not long after the General Election, that a few members of the Cobden Club Committee informally discussed with Mr Thomas Bayley Potter—in his Sussex home, at the Hurst, close by Dunford, Cobden's place of rest and retreat—the question of celebrating in some way, in the midsummer of 1896, the fiftieth anniversary of the Repeal of the Corn Laws. Committee meetings were afterwards held in London; it was decided that there should be some form of commemoration of the jubilee year, and finally it was arranged that the club should hold a special Cobden Club Jubilee Celebration in the usual form of a dinner at the Ship Hotel, Greenwich, coupling the festival with a congratulatory address to the Right Honourable Charles Pelham Villiers, 'the sole survivor of the four statesmen — Peel, Villiers, Cobden and Bright'—to whom the passing of the Bill repealing the Corn Laws was due.

The first choice, the Committee, of a gentleman to take the chair at the banquet, fell upon Viscount Peel, the distinguished son of the great Sir Robert, who received the invitation with great favour, but subsequently, with many expressions of appreciation of the honour, and of the great pleasure it would have given him, regretted that purely personal reasons would prevent him from taking the chair at the banquet on the 26th of June. The Right Honourable Leonard H. Courtney was then invited to take the chair, and graciously accepted the invitation. His admirable and powerful Free Trade speech at the dinner, as corrected by himself, appears in this volume.

The newspaper press, London and provincial, celebrated the jubilee season with exceptional brilliancy, presenting the public with large masses of exceedingly valuable and interesting information on the subject of the Repeal of the Corn Laws, historical, biographical, political and critical.

The conductors of the almost new monthly international review—*Cosmopolis*—which presents its readers, insular and continental, with what is in fact a magazine in three sections—English, French and German—in the three languages, by eminent writers of the three nationalities, marked the occasion by producing a Corn Law Repeal jubilee number for June, with articles on 'The Jubilee of Free Trade' (English), by Henry Dunckley; 'Richard Cobden

(French), by M. Paul Leroy-Beaulieu; and 'A Jubilee of Free Trade and Democracy' (German), by Herr Theodor Barth.

These three Corn Law Repeal jubilee essays form the first three items of the contents of this volume, and this is the first appearance in the English language of the papers by M. Leroy - Beaulieu and Herr Theodor Barth

Since the publication of the article on 'The Jubilee of Free Trade' in the review, the death of Mr Henry Dunckley has deprived the country of one of its most eloquent and brilliant writers on the Free Trade question and the story of Repeal. His own young days were spent in the midst of the conflict. He was personally associated with most of the champions; and in his own way he worked side by side with them. During all these fifty

years there was no man armed with the
pen more able or more ready to take up
the challenge and give an account of the
Free Traders and their work than Mr
Dunckley.

In the opening of his essay Mr Dunckley
speaks of this year's jubilee Cobden Club
banquet as 'a revival probably for this
year only' of the club's old annual dinner,
of which he expresses surprise that it has
'fallen into abeyance.' It is true that the
Cobden Club held its dinner every year,
with four exceptions, from 1866 to 1887;
but it should be understood that the question
of the dinner has always been, in some
degree, dependent upon the pressure of
the club's work upon its resources. For
a while, as we have seen, there was
not the same need that arose later for
setting the printing press in motion on a

large scale for the instruction of the masses of our population in the facts and the doctrine of free exchange. At that time the function of commemoration, in which the club had its origin, and the business of keeping the Free Trade fires burning far and wide in the two hemispheres, were more effectively observed by means of the international Cobden banquet than by any other means. Later on, however, the issue of books, leaflets and pamphlets wherewith to confront reactionary advocacy in its successive forms made large demands on the club's energy and resources, and now and again a club dinner was intermitted in consequence.

M. Paul Leroy-Beaulieu has been long distinguished among French political economists as a Free Trade advocate, but the English economic student will look in vain through

his brilliant but pessimistic essay on 'Richard
Cobden, His Work and the Outcome of His
Ideas,' for any expression of the writer's
faith in Free Exchange as a scientific doctrine. He tells us that Free Trade did not
present itself to Cobden's mind 'simply as a
reasonable arrangement based upon division
of labour and the advantages of international competition,' and then he passes
on, treating Cobden's conception of the
doctrine of Free Trade as merely a
trait of personal character; and one per-
ceives that to M. Leroy - Beaulieu Free
Trade does not go much beyond 'a reasonable arrangement based upon division of
labour,' etc. There is therefore not much
reason to be surprised when, towards the
close of the essay, looking into the future
and asking, 'Will Free Trade eventually
win back the support of the rural classes

and triumph over their opposition?' he has no stronger answer to make than, 'Sooner or later it may be so.' But Adam Smith was not the discoverer, and Richard Cobden was not the apostle, of a mere 'reasonable arrangement.' Mr Cobden could not tell, and none of us can estimate, how long the world will take to realise the irrefragible logic of Free Exchange, but that every rational nation will, at no very distant date, cast off the delusive and suicidal superstition of Protection, no man who has really seen the inside of the problem can for a moment doubt.

We return to solid ground, after the luminous discourse of M. Leroy-Beaulieu, in Herr Theodor Barth's substantial and masterly essay—'A Jubilee of Free Trade and Democracy.' The mournful impression one may gather from M. Leroy-Beaulieu's picturesque portrayal of the failure and disaster which seem to him to have overtaken Richard Cobden's ideas, finds consolation in Herr Barth's simple but convincing demonstration that the reaction, in Europe, America and elsewhere, is not a reaction of principle, but of circumstance. Herr Barth brings us back to the almost mathematical logic of the pure principle and doctrine of Free Trade, and reminds the reader of what his French co-essayist seems for the time to have forgotten — that Protection is only another word for monopoly. He lets us see that political reaction and Protectionist reaction move along side by side and hand in hand. And there are quite fresh and suggestive points in the essay, such as the observation that Protection is a contagious epidemic, disturbing capital all round by reactionary sympathetic influences. Another striking point is that the action of various systems of tariff in different countries interferes with the practical study of the natural phenomena of demand and supply, tending to the mischievous fluctuations consequent upon over-production and under-production. Having gone through Herr Barth's sensible review of the situation, the reader of the two essays will find a special reassurance in this competent German opinion that the Protectionist reaction will not long continue.

Mr Courtney's vigorous speech, covering the whole field of controversy from 1846 to the present hour, and Mr Villiers's intimate and trenchant vindication of the work of Peel and Cobden from the point of view of a full half century of personal retrospect, bring us back to England's own full-hearted Free Trade conviction, and to her triumphant practical solution of the problem, in the face of the nations which are every one of them manifestly suffering, in contrast with ourselves, because they have not believed.

RICHARD GOWING.

LINBANK,
SHORTLANDS,
KENT.

THE JUBILEE OF FREE TRADE

THE JUBILEE OF FREE TRADE

BY HENRY DUNCKLEY, D.C.L.

On the 26th of this present month of June *
fifty years will have passed away since
the Royal assent was given to the Bill
for repealing the duties on corn.

The anniversary is one of some interest,
especially to those who are old enough to
remember the event, and more especially to
the few still living whose memory easily goes
back to the earlier stages of the Anti-Corn
Law Movement, and who may have had
the good fortune to be personally acquainted
with its leaders.   Such was the fortune of

* 1896.

27

the present writer, and this circumstance
may perhaps be admitted as an excuse
should anything in these remarks appear
to go beyond the importance of the occasion.

Soon after the death of Mr Cobden the
Cobden Club was founded, partly for the
purpose of showing respect for his memory,
and partly to assist in the propagation of
his opinions. It is well known that the
person who took the most active part in
the founding of the club, and who has stood
by it in its varying fortunes, is Mr T. B.
Potter, Cobden's successor in the repre-
sentation of Rochdale, who now, from his
house near Midhurst, close to Dunford,
Cobden's old home, finds some solace in preparing for the due celebration of the approaching
anniversary. In the early days of the club
there was a dinner once a year at Greenwich. It was usually held towards the

close of the Parliamentary session, and
seemed to vie in some measure with the
old ministerial whitebait dinner. A special
steamer took the members and their friends
on board at Westminster Bridge, some distinguished man was invited to preside at
the dinner, and the address he delivered
was a prominent feature in the next morning's papers. . A dinner, as M. Thiers
remarked of the Republic in reference to
Frenchmen, is the institution which divides
us the least. It is a fine neutral occasion,
when any differences that may exist are
all forgotten, and a genial catholicity of
feeling prevails. With such an advantage
in its favour it is a wonder that this once
famous dinner should ever have fallen into
abeyance, but so it did. This year there
is to be a revival, probably for this year
only. It will be held, not exactly on the

anniversary of the day which saw the Royal
assent given to the measure of 1846—at such
a time of the year Parliamentary engagements are supreme — but on the day after,
and, as an earnest of what may be expected,
it is enough to say that the Right Hon.
L. H. Courtney has promised to preside.

Of one pleasant feature of the proceedings we are already assured. It is proposed to make some presentation, probably
an address, to the Right Hon. C. P.
Villiers, M.P., as the last survivor of the
four statesmen—Peel, Villiers, Cobden and
Bright—to whom the passing of that measure
was mainly due. There is an obvious pro-
priety in placing Peel's name first. He
was the man who carried the Bill through
the House of Commons. If it had been
brought forward by anyone else its success
would have been impossible. His conver-

sion to the Principle of Free Trade had been the slow work of years, but his misgivings and gradual relentings had, at last, ripened into full conviction. Many who followed him into the lobby were but half convinced. Disraeli had some ground for his sarcasm when he said of the Protectionists, in the course of the debate, that, like the Saxons of old, they ' were converted in battalions and baptized in platoons. It was utterly impossible to bring those individuals from a state of reprobation to a state of grace with a celerity sufficiently quick.' It was Peel's authority with his party that carried the day. The Whigs, who for some years had been clinging to a fixed duty instead of a sliding scale, catching from Cabinet divisions a hint as to the way the wind was blowing, had, at the last moment, spread their sails to the gale by declaring for unconditional repeal, so that their support could be relied upon. In the other House, Peel had the assistance of his old friend and colleague, the Duke of Wellington, who argued the case with a soldier's logic. The Queen's Government must be carried on. This was of more importance than any conceivable question about corn. The Crown and the Commons were in favour of the Bill, and it was not for the Lords to stand out against the other two constituents of Parliament. So the Bill was carried and became law, but Peel had incurred a penalty which was promptly exacted. The very day on which the Royal assent was given to the Bill he was defeated on an Irish measure by a combination of Whigs and Protectionists, the latter panting for revenge, and he was compelled to resign. The

passage referring to Cobden in the speech
announcing his resignation is well known,
but must be quoted here : 'The name,' he
said, 'which ought to be and which will
be associated with the success of these
measures, is the name of a man who, acting, I believe, from pure and disinterested
motives, has advocated their cause with
untiring energy, and by appeals to reason,
expressed by an eloquence the more to
be admired because it was unaffected and
unadorned—the name of Richard Cobden.'

But if Peel's name has a right to stand first
on the list of statesmen to whom the repeal of
the Corn Duties is mainly owing, that of Mr
Villiers may well come next. He is entitled to
the honour of precedence. He was the first
to bring the question before the House of
Commons, and, when he had once begun, he
brought in a motion almost every year, either

for repeal, or with a view to it. The movement with which he was connected had nothing to do with Manchester. 'In 1836,' as Mr Morley tells us, 'the philosophic radicals, including Grote, Molesworth, Hume and Roebuck, had formed an association for repealing the duties on corn. But they did not catch the public ear, and nothing had come of it.' Nevertheless, the fact is not without an interest which may perhaps be described as psychological. These philosophic radicals had no connection with trade. They rather prided themselves upon looking at political questions in the light of pure reason. They condemned the Corn Laws because they regarded them as essentially unjust, the duties being levied—not at all for the sake of the revenue —but solely in the interest of the owners of agricultural land. The duties were, therefore, a tax, nominally paid by importers,

but really paid by the whole community for
the benefit of a small number of its members. The same was true of any other
import duty which had in view the protection of any other interest, and the
argument led at once to the wider question
of Free Trade ; but for the moment it was
the landlords, with the peerage at their
head, who regarded themselves as specially
assailed. Mr Villiers, the brother of the
Earl of Clarendon, belonged to the aristocracy, and for him to take the foremost
place in attacking the duties on corn was
an act open to resentment as a desertion
of his order. In 1841, Cobden entered the
House of Commons as Member for Stock-
port, and at once threw himself, heart and
soul, into the fight. Mr Villiers was never
displaced. Cobden always said he was
proud to serve as his lieutenant, though

his own strenuous fighting qualities, the
great place he filled in the public eye, and
the power he wielded as the representative
of the Anti-Corn Law League, threw his predecessor somewhat into the shade.   There
is a rather pathetic passage on record in
which Cobden avowed his own surprise at
the extent to which the leadership had
become centred in ˙himself, and almost
asked forgiveness for the prominence he
had assumed.   Between two such men
jealousy was out of the question.   It
was enough for them that their cause
triumphed.   Happily Mr Villiers, the survivor of Cobden by more than thirty years,
is still with us to receive his share of the
acknowledgments which are due to both.

But a jubilee implies jubilation, and it
may be asked, What have we to rejoice
over ?   What was there in the measure

which became law fifty years ago that should inspire us with thanksgiving, or make us grateful to the men who helped to place it on the Statute Book?

It might be difficult to convince an obstinate querist on this point, and at any rate we shall make no elaborate attempt. There is hardly a question under heaven on which a scepticism may not exist which no arguments could remove, and anyone who should dispute on a fine day at midsummer whether the sun is shining must be left to his blindness.`

One thing it is almost impossible for us to realise, namely, the actual change which was produced by the passing from a system of Protection to one of Free Trade. That experience belongs to a period from which we are separated by a generation and a half. The new state of things which was then introduced has become natural to us. We are unable to compare the present with the past, since the past has vanished, and we have no knowledge of it, except through books and statistics. We have to realise that Protection was the prop of a bad fiscal system which fettered trade and oppressed the people with taxation, while it made no proportionate returns to the revenue. To assist the imagination, we will take a few sentences from Mr Sydney Buxton's *Finance and Politics*, an invaluable guide to the political student : 'The agricultural interest had, in addition to the practically prohibitive tax on corn, been also protected against the invasion of any other foreign products. Hence the import of all animals, alive or dead, fresh or salted, of their bristles, their hides and their hair, of all vegetables, fruits and seeds

—tares as well as wheat—had been either prohibited or subjected to enormous duties. As an enlightened peer (Lord Radnor) told the House of Lords in 1841, while hundreds and thousands of their countrymen were starving around them, "every animal that walked the earth, nay, every fish which swam, and every bird that was fit for food, must be taxed, lest it should come in cheap for our starving population"' (vol. i. p. 63). The extent to which trade was fettered may be inferred from the number of import duties which at that time were either reduced or repealed. ' Peel found the tariff with over a thousand articles subject to duties, and left it with but half the number: the total number of duties reduced by him was 1035, the total number entirely repealed was 605 — duties for the most part on articles which con-

cerned the food, the clothing, and the comfort of the people, or which, as levied on
the raw material of manufacture, affected
employment' (p. 65). Some industries
which have since become important were
crushed by heavy excise duties, those on
some sorts of glass, for example, being
as much as two hundred per cent. on the
cost price. If they had not been reduced
there would have been no Crystal Palace
in 1851.

These facts may enable us to conceive of
the burdens under which industry laboured
prior to the reforms which ushered in Free
Trade. We add a passage from Mr Wal-
pole's *History*, showing the cost of protection on some of the larger items. 'It was
shown,' he says (vol. iv. p. 132), 'that the
differential duties on foreign and colonial
timber virtually imposed a tax of £2,000,000

a year upon the people ; that the same system raised the price of sugar by 20s. a hundredweight, or, on an average consumption of 4,000,000 cwt., imposed a tax of £4,000,000 on the nation. It was estimated that the average duty on wheat amounted to 10s. a quarter, and that as the people consumed 24,000,000 quarters a year, the bread tax was equivalent to an annual tax of £12,000,000. Protection, therefore, in the case of these three articles was imposing a charge of £18,000,000 on the over-taxed people of this country.' This policy told with disastrous effect upon the condition of the community. Our manufacturers were unable to compete with the produce of other countries, and, where natural advantages might have enabled them to export with a profit, the check put upon imports by a protective tariff prevented them from opening markets abroad. The effect of our import duties was equivalent on our part to a refusal to buy, and as a necessary consequence our own sales were restricted. We did our very best to shut out the foreigner from our market, and we were then perforce shut out from his. The result was that our exports dwindled from year to year; they were smaller in amount in 1842 than they had been in the last year of the great war. As a further result there was diminished employment for the people. Factories everywhere were being closed, and wages were sinking lower and lower. In many cases the workpeople refused to submit, and there were strikes on a great scale. They imagined that the choice of giving them more or less lay with their employers, but the employers were absolutely helpless. The foreign and the home trade were alike impoverished, for food being dear, and all classes in a state of depression, there was no money to spend on articles of any kind that could possibly be dispensed with. These were the circumstances which led to the formation of the Anti - Corn Law League, through whose stupendous efforts, with Cobden as the interpreter of their grievances, the nation was at last aroused. Happily an able and patriotic minister was in power, sufficiently enlightened to comprehend the duties of his position, and endowed with the fortitude requisite to start a new era in the fortunes of the country.*

Now, on behalf of our countrymen who were living a generation and a half ago, we venture to think that the great economical change which was then accomplished is worthy of commemoration. It began at once

* For full statistical evidence of the effect of Free Trade on the condition of the people, see Mr Ralph S. Ashton's Essay on an Imperial Customs Union, published as a supplement to the *Statist* of May 9, 1896.

to work a great improvement in their condition. A feeling of anxiety, which almost
amounted to despair, gave way to hopeful-
ness. Business began to expand, our commerce increased, and there was soon plenty
of employment for everybody. The staple
food of the people was cheapened, and,
whether its price rose or fell, it was no
longer 'leavened with a sense of injustice.'
At the same time, new kinds of food, hitherto
shut out, began to appear in our markets,
and many articles which till then had been
considered luxuries were soon within the
reach of all. So far as we of to-day are
concerned, it is important to remember that
the fiscal reforms begun by Peel were carried
on for the next twenty years, and completed
by Mr Gladstone. Instead of more than a
thousand articles which figured in the customs
tariff of 1842, those on which import duties

are now charged can be reckoned on one's fingers, and, if alcoholic liquors are excluded, on the fingers of one hand. The effect of these further changes in diminishing the cost of food and clothing, and in multiplying the comforts of the people, is open to general observation, but their most important result is the freedom given to trade.

So far as other nations will permit us, we are ready to exchange productions with them. No obstacle is offered on our part. Our ports and markets are open to all; and, in spite of the high tariffs which they have set up for the purpose of keeping us out of theirs, the great market which lies open within our shores is a temptation which cannot be resisted, and directly or indirectly they have to take payment in the produce of our labour. Ours is a cosmopolitan position, and it is one which our large and growing population, so disproportionate to the comparatively small area of these islands, forces us to occupy.

The policy of the last fifty years is justified by the results. On the whole it cannot be doubted that the period has been one of steady improvement. Taking such tests as the rate of wages paid to all classes of work-people, the purchasing power of their wages, the standard of comfort they have reached, the spread of education, the growth of self-help in societies of all kinds, but especially in the great co-operative associations which have come into existence, the sanitary condition of our towns, the provision made for recreation in public parks, gardens and museums, the enormously diminished proportions of pauperism and crime, or whatever other tests one may choose to select, the contrast between 'now and then' is perhaps

the greatest that can be found in the whole
course of our history. What depth the nation
would have reached if it had gone on sinking
as it was doing just before the Free Trade
reforms began, we are happily not permitted
to know. It is enough that we were saved,
and that a new lease of prosperous existence
was in store for us. It seems but reasonable that we should think gratefully of this
surprising change, and of the men who were
the means of bringing it about. The members
of the Cobden Club have on the whole a
very sufficient apology for their jubilee.

In connection with any great change, however beneficent, there usually springs up a
crop of gainsayers, who are ready to insist,
in spite of the clearest evidence, that it is
not at all so great or so beneficent as its
authors held it to be, and that for the most
part it is probably a delusion. Those who

pose under more or less specious disguises
as the opponents of Free Trade make it
their chief topic of reproach that other
nations have not followed our example, and
they quote some sanguine expressions of Mr
Cobden as a proof that his foresight was at
fault, and that his prophecies, as they style
them, remain unfulfilled.   It is true that Cobden, in the enthusiasm of his convictions,
took a more hopeful view of the immediate
future of Europe and of the world than
events have since warranted.   In 1846 we
had enjoyed thirty years of almost uninter-
rupted peace, and there appeared to be a
reasonable prospect of its continuance.   Had
the hopes then entertained been fulfilled,
international commerce might have fared
better.   But it was not to be.   The demon
of war was soon abroad to plague the nations,
and industry had to bear the strain.   But it

certainly is not true, as has been alleged, that Cobden would not have recommended us to adopt Free Trade for ourselves if he had foreseen that our example would not be generally imitated, and that at the end of fifty years we should be the only great nation in the world avowedly adopting as its policy an unrestricted exchange of commodities. The principle he laid down was that, whatever course other nations might choose to take, a policy of Free Trade was always the best. It appeared to him that the refusal of other nations to buy from us on equal terms was no reason in the world why we should refuse to buy from them. Buying and selling are but two sides of one and the same transaction, and if we managed to buy from them, it is certain that they would be obliged, directly or indirectly, to buy from us in return. The high duties imposed by their tariffs would be paid by their own people on every article imported; and, though the the effect would be to make the business done with them by our manufacturers and merchants less profitable than it would be if done on more equal terms, there would still be some profit, or the transaction would not take place. Free Trade on both sides would be far better, but half a loaf is better than no bread. We cannot force other nations to adopt what seems to us a wise policy, but that is no reason why we should adopt a foolish one, or why we should decline to make a small profit rather than none at all.

Peel recognised this doctrine, and acted upon it. In the speech with which he introduced his chief Free Trade measure, he said: 'I fairly avow to you that in making this great reduction on the import of articles, the produce and manufactures of foreign countries, I have no guarantee to give you that other countries will immediately follow our example. Wearied with our long and unavailing efforts to enter into satisfactory commercial treaties with other nations, we have resolved at length to consult our own interests, and not to punish those other countries for the wrong they do us in continuing their high duties upon the importation of our products and manufactures. We have had no communication with any foreign Government upon the subject of these reductions. We cannot promise that France will immediately make a corresponding reduction in her tariff. We cannot promise that Russia will prove her gratitude to us for our reduction of duty on her tallow by any diminution of her duties. You may ask, therefore; why this superfluous liberality, that you are going to do away with all these duties, and yet you expect nothing in return?' He even had to admit that, during the four years over which his previous relaxations of the tariff had extended, some foreign nations had levied higher duties on our goods. But he points to the fact that during those same four years our exports, after having been stationary or declining for a quarter of a century, had increased by as much as ten millions. How had this come to happen? To some extent we had benefited by the services of the smuggler, whose business flourishes on high duties. Then the cost of Protection, the heavy taxation it involved, had disqualified the foreigner for competing with us successfully, while the repeal of duties on the raw materials of our manufactures had given a fresh impetus to skill and industry, and enabled us to defy competition in neutral markets. As regards the future, Peel had no sanguine expectations, though his belief was that in the course of time the 'sense of the people, of the great body of consumers,' would bring about a relaxation of high duties. 'I trust,' he said in conclusion, 'that this improved intercourse with foreign countries will constitute a new bond of peace, and that the lovers of peace between nations will derive material strength from the example which I have advised, by remitting the impediments to commercial intercourse.'

The hope expressed in these closing lines has not been fulfilled, and an explanation which, whether or not the true one, is at anyrate adequate, can be assigned.

It has already been remarked that in 1846, when these words were uttered, Europe had enjoyed thirty years of peace. During the next thirty years there were six great wars, and they were preceded by the general convulsion of 1848. The space between the election of Louis Napoleon as Prince President of the French Republic and his assuming imperial rank was anything but a quiet time. The Crimean War followed soon after, and the treaty by which that war was concluded gave no obscure intimation of another which broke out three years later, with France and Sardinia as allies against Austria. A couple of years more bring us to the Schleswig-Holstein disputes, with the war of the Duchies, into which we were very nearly drawn, leading on to the Austro-Prussian War of 1866. The next four years were spent in expectancy of a greater conflict which it was clear could not be long delayed, and which burst upon us in 1870. The Germans had hardly evacuated France, when troubles began on the Danube. Eventually there was the war between Russia and Turkey, at which the other Powers in some measure 'assisted.' It is a long time since Europe witnessed such a series of wars within the limits of a quarter of a century. What chance was there, while these conflicts were going on, for the peaceful development of commerce along Free Trade lines? These great wars had one aggregate result which threw another difficulty in the way of a general reduction of tariffs. The Continental Powers increased their armaments on an enormous scale. What with the cost of actual wars and the cost of maintaining vast armies in a state of constant readiness for war, the

Governments have had no money to spare.
They have rather had to take precautions
against an empty Treasury, and the maintenance of high duties seemed to be among the
proper means of preventing such a calamity.
Perhaps a more subtle evil has been en-
gendered.   Nations have been learning to
suspect and dislike each other.   The passions
of war have been transferred to the domain
of industry and trade.   They are jealous of
each other's progress, and fight over commercial concessions as they would over so
many square miles of territory.   One of
the greatest of all wars must not be forgotten—the American Civil War of 1860.
It entailed an enormous debt which became
substantially a charge upon foreign commerce.

It must be admitted that if other nations
have not followed our example, reasons
can be given for their failure.   The course

of events has been unfavourable. Almost
incessant war, with the financial burdens
it involved, has been fatal to any better
prospects of which there may have been
a possibility. Perhaps there were none from
the beginning. In any case the expediency
of the policy we have adopted remains the
same. We adopted it with our eyes open.
We did so at a time when there was no
sign that it would be reciprocated. After
having sought in vain to enter into satisfactory commercial treaties, we gave up
the attempt, and resolved, as Peel observed,
'to consult our own interests.' It is sometimes said that by becoming Free Traders
we have 'given everything away,' and have
nothing left with which to make a bargain. Lord Salisbury has pleaded this point
pathetically. But there was a time when
we had plenty to give away. Our tariff

was protective from top to bottom, and we were in a position to make concessions to any country that might be willing to make an adequate return. We abandoned he idea of reciprocity only when experience had shown that it was impracticable, and that the best hopes of an expanding and progressive commerce lay in the adoption of Free Trade.

Yet, as is well known, we did make a commercial treaty long after we had finally committed ourselves to the principle of Free Trade, and Cobden was the chief negotiator. The French Treaty of 1860 stands before us like a broken column, some will perhaps say, as much a warning as a guide. It may be said to have originated with the eminent French economist, M. Michel Chevalier, one of Cobden's friends, and, like him, an ardent free-trader. In the autumn of 1859 he suggested to Cobden that the Emperor might not be unfavourable to a revision of the tariff in the sense of reducing the duties which told most heavily upon British manufactures, and that we were in a position to offer some inducement by undertaking to reduce the duties on French wines. It happened that wine and brandy had been left untouched by our fiscal reforms, possibly on the chance that they might some day come in useful as a basis of negotiation with our French neighbours, and it seemed to Cobden that an attempt in that direction might well be made. It was obvious that in making it there would be some departure from the strict principle of Free Trade. It would be a return to the reciprocity system which had been avowedly abandoned. But Cobden knew how to safeguard our policy on this point.

Whatever changes might have to be made in our customs duties with a view to meet the wishes of France, he had no intention that they should be made for France alone. To reduce them would clearly be a further step in the direction of Free Trade, and if we reduced them absolutely, so that other nations, as well as France, should have the benefit of them, any objection on the score of principle would seem to be avoided. There was one important fact which should perhaps have received more consideration than it did. The French people were strenuously opposed to Free Trade. Cobden himself admitted that 'it would hardly be possible to assemble five hundred persons together (in France) by any process of selection, and not find nine-tenths of them at least in favour of the present restrictive system.' The con-

stitution entrusted the Emperor with the
treaty - making power. He could therefore
make a commercial treaty with Great Britain
without having to seek the assent of the
Legislature. It is likely that, when this
power was accorded to the Emperor, it
hardly occurred to anybody that it might
be used for the purpose of re-arranging
the commercial relations of France with
foreign countries, but there it was, to be
used for any purpose the Emperor thought
fit. As an advanced Liberal, Cobden had
no liking for Imperialism in any shape, but
if scruples occurred to him, he reflected, and
indeed said, that the French had a right
to make what laws they pleased; that if
they had decided to give this power to the
Emperor, it was not for a foreigner to raise
objections, and that as he had been virtually elected by the nation as a whole, and by

universal suffrage, he might be considered as possessing a representative authority superior to that of the Legislature. But, as events proved, this was the weak point of the treaty. Cobden no doubt hoped that if the treaty were once made it would have such a beneficial effect upon French commerce as to reconcile the French to any flaws in its origin; but in this he was mistaken.

No doubt there was something especially tempting to Cobden in the idea of entering into negotiations with the Emperor, with a view to effecting, through him, commercial changes which would bring his country and ours closer together and promote the cause of peace. This cause was dear to him. To promote it was one of the great aims of his life. It may be difficult to say whether he was more attached to com-

mercial freedom because it would tend to
promote peace, or to a peaceful policy
because it would tend to promote commercial freedom. His views were never
confined to England. His earliest writings,
the very first of his utterances as a politician, had for their subject the international
relations of this country, and a largeness
of vision which took the whole world
within its ken was perhaps his most prominent characteristic. Needless to say, he
was a thorough Englishman, true to the
traditions and sentiments which he inherited
as the descendant of a race of Sussex
yeomen, and never more at home than
when in company with farmers, discussing
the state of their crops. But he had an
abiding conviction that there was no antagonism between the interests of one nation
and those of another, and that every

trading transaction, every exchange of commodities, had in it a double benefit, and
was necessarily advantageous to both parties.
The largest commercial intercourse between
two nations, or between all nations put
together, was but the aggregate of transactions which were singly and separately
beneficial to all concerned. Cobden was
especially anxious to see a good under-
standing established between Great Britain
and France, and it seemed to him that no
better means could be devised, with a view
to the accomplishment of this object, than
the relaxation of those commercial restrictions which kept them apart. Acting on
the suggestion he had received from a
good Frenchman, he sounded some of the
Government officials, and at last discussed
the subject with the Emperor, doing so
with the knowledge and assent of our

Foreign Office, but without any express authorisation. The Emperor was more favourable to the scheme than those upon whose advice he usually relied. He was supposed to have some leanings towards Free Trade ; but the motives which influenced him were probably political, partly perhaps a desire to make a good impression on English opinion, and partly a hope that an extension of French trade would increase his popularity with his own people, especially in the vine-growing districts of the south. The encouragement thus afforded, together with the influence of Mr Gladstone and Mr Bright, induced the Government to enter into negotiations. The following year Cobden and Lord Cowley, the British Ambassador at Paris, were commissioned to conduct them, and after an unparalleled amount of labour, extending

E

through the year, and of which the chief burden fell upon Cobden, the treaty was concluded.

The treaty had an immediate success. The aggregate trade between the two countries, including imports and exports, which just before had been less than twenty millions annually, amounted in five years to sixty-three and a half millions. Unfortunately these happen to be almost the precise figures for 1894, the latest published. The treaty was 'denounced' in 1872 by M. Thiers, who decribed it as a 'deplorable yoke on the nation'; but M. Léon Say became his Finance Minister towards the close of the year, and it is perhaps due to his influence that no change was then made. The treaty remained substantially in force till 1880, when the French Government proposed to make a new one, and

M. Léon Say was sent over as ambassador
to conduct the negotiations in London.
His reputation as an economist and free-
trader secured him a warm welcome, but
he returned a month later on being chosen
President of the Senate. His successor was
M. Challemell-Lacour, who in a conversation with Lord Granville said 'that he
was no doubt a free-trader, a *libre-échangiste*,
but that he was a *libre-échangiste Fran-
çais*, and recognised the necessity of paying due consideration to the interests of
national industries.' This very clearly de-
fined his position, and also explained the
object which the French Government had
in view in wishing to make a new treaty.
They proposed a higher scale of duties, and
the substitution of specific for *ad valorem*
duties. This latter proposal was especially
objectionable, since specific duties tell un-

fairly upon articles of British manufacture, one of whose recommendations is their comparative cheapness. The English Commissioners at Paris, Sir Charles Dilke, Sir C. Rivers Wilson, Mr W. E. Baxter, and Mr Kennedy, were busily at work for a year and a half, assisted by experts from Manchester, Bradford, and other manufacturing centres ; but it was found impossible to agree, and the British Government wisely decided to be free from all engagements rather than accept the only treaty which there was any chance of framing.

The French Government were in the meantime engaged in arranging a general tariff which should supersede all existing treaties, but be open to remission in special cases. The British Government asked to be placed on the footing of 'the most favoured nation,' but this was refused, unless a promise were given that the existing duties on our French imports should not be increased, and this proposal was declined. There was some little tension of feeling, but a Bill soon after passed the Legislature conceding 'the most favoured nation' treatment to Great Britain.

Such has been the fate of this famous treaty. It should be remembered, as a fact which may have had some influence on French policy, that a clause was inserted in the Treaty of Frankfort stipulating that Germany should always be on a footing with 'the most favoured nation,' so that the concessions we sought in 1880, if they had been made to us, must also have been made to Germany. A general tariff was more in harmony with French ideas, and it is as well that we have regained our freedom. But whatever objections, theoretic or academic, may have been urged against the French treaty, there can be no doubt that it has exerted a useful influence in many ways. While it lasted, the relations between England and France were more friendly and more stable than they had been for many years before; and, in spite of recent rivalries, we may hope that the better feeling which the two nations were led to cultivate is not quite extinguished. The effect it has had upon international commerce cannot be more lucidly summed up than in the words of Mr Sydney Buxton in the work to which we have already been indebted. 'Free Trade,' he says, 'has not indeed been adopted by other nations, but the negotiation of the French Commercial Treaty set a good example. Treaty has followed treaty, not only between England and other nations, but between those nations themselves, until Europe and most of the world is covered with a network of fiscal agreements. These, and especially the extension of the most favoured nation system, by means of which an international advantage given to one is given to all, if they have not indeed brought Free Trade, or even made for Free Trade, have had a lasting effect in lowering custom tariffs, and in encouraging international trade. Such an impulse has thereby been given to trade that even the tendency to increase protective duties which has of late manifested itself abroad, has not succeeded in counteracting the improvement that took place in the years immediately succeeding 1860 in the fiscal system of the world.'

The treaty achieved this success because it harmonised with current opinions. It fell in with the passion for chaffering and higgling which belongs from of old to the mercantile temperament. It seemed to grant that a lowering of duties involved something of loss and sacrifice which could only be justified in consideration of a full equivalent given in return. It remains to be seen whether the further lesson will be learned that an exchange of commodities must always be profitable or it would not take place, and that to afford all possible facilities for exchange is the surest way of promoting the common interests of all countries.

Whether we are within a 'measurable distance' from a period of universal Free Trade, or whether it will ever come at all, is a question which may as well be left for the present in the region of conjecture. Producers everywhere are naturally disposed to welcome restrictions which, by screening them from competition, enable them to make larger profits, and through their superior wealth and influence they catch most easily the ear of governments. That their interests are identical with those of the nation is simply a pleasant fiction which they succeed in imposing upon public opinion. The great body of consumers do not see that the higher profits made by Protection are made at their expense; that they pay the money out of their own pockets in the higher prices of food and clothing. The national sentiment is pressed into service as an ally. Emblems and epithets are borrowed from the field of battle. The war of tariffs is waged like a war for territory, and when it is asked with an air of patriotism whether the foreigner shall be allowed to beard us in our own markets, popular prejudice may be expected to answer with a resounding 'No.' It will take a long time for sounder views to spread, and very little can be done to quicken the process. Anything in the shape of advice from another nation is viewed with suspicion, and is resented. Every nation must be left to form its own judgment as to what is best for its own interests, with experience as its sole teacher. This is the course we took fifty years ago, when we committed ourselves to the policy of Free Trade, and our example, steadfastly maintained, is the most effectual and the most inoffensive method we can employ for commending that policy to the world.

RICHARD COBDEN: HIS WORK AND
THE OUTCOME OF HIS IDEAS

RICHARD COBDEN:

His Work and the Outcome of His Ideas.

BY PAUL LEROY-BEAULIEU

I

THE career of Cobden was both original and reproductive. The son of a small Sussex farmer who had fallen upon evil days, he spent his early youth as a warehouse clerk. After a while, he exchanged this sedentary occupation for the post of a commercial traveller, making journeys by coach through different parts of the country at the rate of about forty miles a day, collecting accounts and soliciting orders for muslins and calicoes. Subsequently, in partnership with a couple of friends, none of them possessing as much as two hundred pounds, he established a London agency for the sale of cotton goods. Meanwhile he bought books, set himself to learn Latin, and made a voyage to America, which deeply impressed him, and for which, unlike the generality of Englishmen, in his day he conceived a warm admiration. He also visited Greece and passed the following judgment on that country: 'What famous puffers those old Greeks were! Half the educated world in Europe is now devoting more thought to the ancient affairs of these Lilliputian states, the squabbles of their tribes, the wars of their villages, the geography of their rivulets and hillocks, than they bestow upon the modern history of the South and North Americas, the politics of the United States, and the charts of the mighty rivers and mountains of the new world.' Egypt,

Asia Minor, Russia, were also visited by this close observer, whose mind was altogether engrossed in the new age, bent on gauging and preparing for the future,

He lived, worked, and influenced his fellow men as though he had been inspired. He was a man of ideas, who, mindful of his early days, under pressure of his circumstances and his calling, devoted every thought and effort to practical reforms. He was never in the service of the Government; he did not become a Minister like his friend Bright. His whole force, which was considerable, he drew from himself, from the fervour of his soul, his speech and his writings. As in his youth he had travelled in muslins and calicoes, so during the rest of his life he travelled, as it were, in political and social ideas with endless speeches, meetings, pamphlets and letters.

His programme included but a few simple items: Free Trade first of all, as became an English democrat trained to business; popular education; the levelling down of the territorial party; and peace — not perhaps universal peace but at least a peace for Great Britain — to be obtained by systematic non - intervention in Continental affairs, and, if that were possible, the abandonment of England's colonial policy. Cobden had no doubt as to the right method of carrying this programme into effect. It was to be done by incessant agitation, and by the association of all who wished well to their fellow men. If these weapons occasionally failed, that was because the men who wielded them had not made the best use of them. He called for an army of lecturers and a deluge of tracts as an antidote for the poison with which the mind of the people had been filled. He frequently urged that Fox, in order to prevent the war of 1793, had not been ashamed to call on his friends to promote meetings in the counties, and to send petitions from the Quakers and others to the House of Commons. Though he disliked all religious intolerance, the work of the Society of Friends delighted him. He magnified as heroes, in an order of the day, the philanthropists who carried assistance to the Irish mowed down by famine and by the diseases which follow in its train. 'Here,' said he, 'was courage. No music strung the nerves; no smoke obscured the imminent danger; no thunder of artillery deadened the senses. It was cool self-possession and resolute will; calculating risk and heroic resignation. And who were these brave men? To what gallant corps did they belong? Were they of

F

the horse, foot, or artillery force? They were Quakers from Clapham and Kingston! If you would know what heroic actions they performed, you must inquire from those who witnessed them. You will not find them recorded in the volume of reports published by themselves—for Quakers write no bulletins of their victories.' Cobden's biographer, Mr John Morley, one of the leaders of modern Liberalism, declares that the passage from which these words are taken is amongst the finest examples of English prose, not only for its genuine sentiments, but also for the vigour, simplicity and loftiness of its expression.

Cobden was an apostle; he lifted all the interests of humanity into a higher sphere, where they ceased to be mere questions of circumstance, and became bound up with immutable principles. Free Trade did not present itself to his mind simply as a reasonable arrangement based upon division of labour and the advantages of international competition; it was the international law of the Almighty; and it was not sufficient for the triumph of this divine law to appeal to the intellect. The heart must be elevated. 'I think the scattered elements [of the Liberal party] may yet be rallied,' he wrote to his brother Frederick in 1838, 'round the question of the Corn Laws. *It appears to me that a moral, and even a religious spirit may be infused into that topic, and if agitated in the same manner that the question of slavery has been, it will be irresistible.*' These few lines, which his biographer prints in italics, are a complete portrait of the man.* What an utter mistake that was of M. Pouyer-Quertier,

---

* The long biography which Mr Morley has devoted to Cobden, and of which Mdlle. Sophie Raffalovitch (Mrs

who was wont to speak of Cobden as *rusé !*
Never was there a character with less of
cunning, or one more instinctive, more
simple, more artless in the best sense, and
more open. He could neither make a fortune nor keep that which was created for
him by free-will offerings. He declined
Mr Gladstone's offer to make him President,
with a high salary, of a sort of British
Court of Accounts.*

No one used less of flattery to the
people ; more than once he set himself in
opposition to its enthusiasms, as in the
case of the Crimean War, and again when
English public opinion appeared to side
with the Confederate States against the

O'Brien) has given us a fine translation, is of the utmost
interest for such as would understand the psychological
character of a considerable section of the English Liberal
party, if not of that party as a whole.

* The Board of Audit. The offer was made and declined
in 1865.—*Tr.*

North, during the long war of secession.
'I will never,' he said, in a speech delivered in 1855, 'truckle so low to the
popular spirit of the moment as to join in
any cry which shall divert the mass of the
people from what I believe should be their
first thought and consideration, namely, how
far they themselves are responsible for the
evils which may fall upon the land, and
how far they should begin at home before
they begin to find fault with others.' Opposing alike the Whigs and the Tories,
Cobden was, it must be allowed, quite a
special sort of Radical.

II

Cobden had two great triumphs in his
life—one almost at the beginning of his
career in 1846: the abolition of the Corn
Laws, a collective work in which he took

the principal part; the other, near the end of his life—the reform of international commercial relations. Strangely enough, he was not the initiator of this movement. The Commercial Treaty of 1860, between England and France, is in the former country universally called the Cobden Treaty, just as the treaty of 1786, which had the same object, and between the same two nations, is called the Eden Treaty. The fact is that the treaty of 1860 ought to be called the Michel Chevalier Treaty. It is not contested that this economist, as ardent an agitator as Cobden, and possessing the confidence of the Emperor, suggested to Cobden and Gladstone, on a journey to London in 1859, the idea of a treaty with France. Cobden welcomed this idea. From the association of two men who had no part in the Government of either England or

France, and who were both of them what M. Rouher once called, though without thinking of either, ' individualities without a mandate,' sprang not merely the celebrated treaty of commerce between England and France, but also the thoroughly Liberal reform of international commercial relations amongst the chief civilised countries.

This was for Cobden a triumph which did more than anything else to engrave his name on the hearts of Englishmen, and connected it with an historical act of primary importance. It would be superfluous to examine in detail the clauses of the treaty of 1860, the abandonment of prohibition, the establishment of a moderate tariff, mostly from ten to fifteen per cent., on the value of foreign produce imported into France, a corresponding abatement of the wine duty in England, and the enor-

mous increase of trade between the two
countries.   Other nations followed suit, such
as Prussia, Italy, Austria, Switzerland and
Belgium.   One might have thought that
by these manifold commercial conventions
the world was advancing towards absolute
Free Trade.

In other spheres of his activity, Cobden
had been less fortunate; public opinion in
England was not so easily influenced by
his other doctrines.   Having a deep faith
in the freedom of humanity, all he asked
of the Government was to smooth away
the obstacles which made it difficult to approach.   The Socialistic Radicals were still
unknown.   Cobden had never allied himself with them.   He belonged entirely to
what has since been called the Manchester
School; or, rather, he may be said to
have founded it.   He never liked the in-

tervention of the State in labour questions, except for the protection of children. In 1836, during his first unsuccessful Parliamentary contest, he declared (to use Mr Morley's words) 'that for plain physical reasons no child ought to be put to work in a cotton mill so early as the age of thirteen, but whatever restrictions on the hours of labour might be desirable, it was not for the legislature to impose them; it was for the workmen to insist upon them, relying not on Parliament, but on their own action.' Nearly thirty · years afterwards, at the height of his reputation and influence, he opposed in Parliament the wide extension of manufacturing establishments under Government control. He maintained that the State ought not to produce for itself what it could obtain from private producers. This was the subject of his last speech in the House of Commons.

His whole life was full of keen criticism of a growing expenditure, especially on the Army and Navy. No one was more opposed to what are now called imperial politics. He could not see the value of the colonies; and it must be confessed that on this point his ideas were wanting in breadth and justice. If one could only have Free Trade with a barbarous or half barbarous country, he thought that nothing better could be desired. He forgot that, in order to develop the resources of any country, we must have preliminary conditions of security and justice, vast capital and skilful organisation, a whole host of provisions which, in certain climates and with certain races, can only be secured by imposing the political authority of the

Western nations. He would gladly have
put an end to colonisation, instead of improving and modifying its methods. He felt
no sort of need for a Greater Britain; he
would gladly have assisted to confine the
power of England to the two British Isles,
or even to Great Britain alone. With much
energy he blamed the first war against
Burmah, denouncing the expedition as arro-
gant, unjust and foolish. A scheme for the
fortification of Canada exasperated him. He
did not even favour the retention of India.

Nothing could equal the vigour of his
repeated statement that England is per-
forming in India a work opposed to morality
and to the nature of things. 'I am,' he said,
'and always have been of opinion that we
have attempted an impossibility in giving
ourselves ·to the task of governing one
hundred millions of Asiatics.' (To-day he

would have had to say two hundred millions.)
'God and his visible natural laws have opposed
insuperable obstacles to the success of such
a scheme. . . . I can't even co-operate with
those who seek to "reform" India, for I have
no faith in the power of England to govern
that country at all permanently. . . . There
is no future but trouble and loss and disappointment, and, I fear, crime in India;
and they are doing the people of this
country the greatest service who tell them
the honest truth according to their convictions, and prepare them for abandoning at
some future time the thankless and impossible
task.' * It was in 1858, at the height of the
Sepoy rebellion, that Cobden thus entertained
the idea of abandoning Hindostan ; and he
did not give up the idea after the re-estab-

* Letter to Mr Ashworth, from Midhurst, Oct. 16, 1857.
Morley's *Life*, Jubilee Edition, ii. 206.

lishment of the *pax Britannica* in this vast
region. In August 1860 he wrote again :—
'I have no heart for discussing any of the
details of Indian management, for I look on
our rule there, as a whole, with an eye of
despair. . . . Ultimately, of course, nature
will assert the supremacy of her laws, and
the white-skins will withdraw to their own
latitudes, leaving the Hindoos to the enjoyment of the climate to which their complexion
is suited. . . . It is from an abiding conviction in my mind that we have entered upon
an impossible and hopeless career in India,
that I can never bring my mind to take an
interest in the details of its government.'*

Cobden was haunted by the fear that an
attempt would be made to carry on the
same work, so chimerical in his eyes, in
China. An expedition against that country,

* Letter to William Hargreaves, from Paris, Aug. 4, 1860.

or the bombardment of its ports, whatever might be the cause of these proceedings, appeared to him as madness and cruelty. In one of his last speeches he returned to this subject in greater detail, and in quite a dogmatic vein. He strove to show that the demand for new markets may become as dangerous as the old cry for new possessions. The vast growth of industry, he said, makes one section of the commercial class as anxious to employ force in order to open new outlets for its activity as the aristocracy had been to pander to national pride or military ambition. His biographer, Mr Morley, adds, or at least added in 1881, that Cobden's exposure of the dangers which menace us on this side has as much practical application to-day as at that moment.

The national ideal of Cobden was that England should become a greater Belgium, safe against all dangers by its insular position, forming commercial treaties with all nations. He could scarcely see the use of a Navy. At anyrate, he waged bitter war against increasing votes for this service.

III

Thirty-one years have passed away since the death of this untiring, and, in a great measure, successful apostle of the ideas of Free Trade, popular education and peace. We may ask ourselves to-day what are the definite results of that unceasing energy, that indefatigable agitation. Even if the work of Cobden had been merely ephemeral, or if it had lasted no more than two or three decades, it could not have been said to be absolutely fruitless. When one man has induced his country, and, for the matter of that, several countries, to take a new and successful course for a quarter of a century, he has an ample reward for his labours, and we ought clearly to acknowledge their efficacy.

Is the work of Cobden effaced to-day? So far as popular education is concerned, England has adhered to the policy which he advocated. Yet it may be that the fruits of national education are not exactly what Cobden expected it to bear. The development of Socialistic ideas in Great Britain, a constant demand for the intervention of the State, the extension of Municipal, if not of State industries, are in marked contrast with the ideas maintained by the member for Rochdale, and especially with his last speech in Parliament, a few months before he died. The widening of the franchise, so as to include a large new electorate, has not conferred on the United Kingdom that sober and moderate form of government, free from extravagant excitement and from political quackery, to which the Radical idealists of 1837 and 1860 had looked forward. Assuredly it would astonish Cobden to find Jingoism and Toryism so much in vogue as they are at this moment. A general election such as that of 1895 would hopelessly puzzle him. The man who had striven so ardently against what he called the 'Three Panics,' and who, as his biographer says, had told the humiliating story of the inconsistent fears of invasion which had seized in turn upon three Ministries, in 1848, in 1853, and in 1862, would be astounded to see England once more harbouring alarms of this kind. The man who spoke about giving a 'slap in the face' to the dangerous madmen who were for ever raising the cry of a French invasion, would resent as humiliating the opposition of his country, prolonged for nearly twenty years, to a work so pacific, and so favourable to civilisation, as the sub-marine railway between England and France, which was advocated by his friend, Michel Chevalier.

In one particular, Cobden gained a definite triumph. Since the question of the Duchies in 1864, England has not intervened in continental affairs. But how much he would have been concerned over the expansion of colonial politics, and of that Imperialism which he had done all he could to nip in the bud! He was spared from witnessing the proclamation of Queen Victoria as Empress of India, after declaring, as we have seen above, that the supremacy of England in Hindostan filled him with a sense of despair. The systematic renewal of Chartered Companies, British aggression in the South and Central Africa,

the harsh suppression of Matabele revolts or
of the opposition in Uganda, would have
seemed in his eyes but madness and cruelty,
as he said of the far more legitimate war
in China. The raid of Jameson upon a
friendly territory, the enthusiastic welcome
given to the raider in England, who only
escaped death by the clemency of his con-
querors, would have caused him to renew
his familiar note of indignation. 'The world,'
he wrote to Mr Thomasson in 1852,* 'never
yet knew so warlike and aggressive a people
as the British. I wish to see a map on
Mercator's projection published, with a red
spot to mark the places on sea and land
where bloody battles have been fought by
Englishmen. It would be found that, unlike
every other people, we have during seven
centuries been fighting with foreign enemies

* Morley's *Life*, ii. 132-3.

everywhere excepting on our own soil. Need
another word be said to prove us the most
aggressive race under the sun?' And in
regard to India, he spoke of 'those bloody
annals for which God will assuredly exact
a retribution from us or our children.' This
gentle man sought in vain to 'put down the
warlike spirit of our countrymen.' He took
some comfort from ascribing it to the omni-
potence of the aristocracy. The spirit must
be allayed by convincing Englishmen, 'that
their energies have been perverted to a
disastrous course, so far as *their* interests
are concerned, by a ruling class which has
reaped all the honours and emoluments, while
the nation inherits the burdens and respon-
sibilities. Our modern history must be re-
written.' But if he were living to-day, this
apostle of mercy, so full of confidence in the
wisdom and humanity of the people, would

not find it in his power to make the aristocracy responsible for the ardent zeal of the
Briton for colonial conquest.

Indeed, it is a question whether there is
anywhere in Great Britain an isolated spot in
which Cobden, if he were to come back to
earth, could make his home in the midst of
a calm, peaceful and fair-minded population,
governed by the laws of reason and equity.
How would it be in the city of Manchester,
for instance, which has given its name to the
school of private initiative, self-help, mistrust
of State intervention, voluntary and progressive reform without compulsion, and which
has long been the home of that '*Man-
chesterthum*' to which the German academic Socialists have been so keenly hostile?
By a strange mental revolution, the Manchester of to-day is the very birthplace of
economic reaction in Great Britain; Fair

Trade or Reciprocity is advocated there instead of Free Trade; they make a point of preventing India, in her financial depression, from placing a light fiscal duty of five per cent. on English cotton goods; they are beginning to talk about bimetallism, or the artificial increase of money, as a stimulus of trade. If there were an election at this moment in Manchester, and the candidates were Cobden, the apostle of Free Trade and peace, and against him Mr Balfour, pledged to an imperial policy and economic nostrums, the betting would be in favour of the second, and there would be very little doubt as to the result.

The soul of Cobden might make a long pilgrimage in Great Britain without finding a single town which had remained faithful to his principles as a whole. Rochdale, perhaps, would still give him a good reception, though it is not certain that even at Rochdale he would not have to modify his programme, at anyrate, on social lines. He would probably have to take refuge amongst a small society of persevering agitators like the Cobden Club; although, at the last meeting of members, or the last but one, this society, founded in his honour, to perpetuate his doctrines and to venerate his name, it was deemed impossible to discuss the question of bimetallism for fear of creating a schism!

Everywhere else, except amongst this group of friends, Cobden would find his work in danger. Some there are who cry up Imperial Federation, which would lead, at anyrate, to a partial revival of the old colonial system of differential duties in favour of colonial products. An economic journal like the *Statist* offers a prize of a thousand guineas for the best essay on a plan of this kind.* Others call for Government grants in relief of agriculture; and the Budget of the current year, 1896-7, devotes more than a million sterling to various kinds of agricultural aid.

Again, if Cobden were to look beyond his own country, and take note of foreign nations, he would perceive on every hand the triumph of Protection and Jingoism in close alliance. In the United States, a democracy which seemed to him like a pioneer for others of the same kind, he would see M'Kinley, with his duties of 50 and 75 per cent., the favourite candidate for the presidency; in France he would see arbitrary tariffs springing up on the ruins of the commercial treaties; and even in Belgium, an exclusively industrial nation, which cannot produce

* See an article on April 18th, 1896, and in other numbers during the previous twelvemonth, on an 'Imperial Customs Union.'

food for its own population, he would find duties imposed on a number of agricultural products.

Cobden would indeed be troubled by this return to the old customs, which he had reason to think abandoned for ever. And yet he had never been thoroughly confident on this point; he did not possess the sanguine temperament of Michel Chevalier. Full of impatience at the slow progress of reform in France, he wrote to Chevalier in 1864 :—'I confess I am sorry when I see that you do not introduce new reforms, even if it were only as a guarantee against reaction from those which have already been secured. Time presses. It is four years since we regulated the tariff. Are you sure that in 1870 you will be under a state of things sufficiently favourable to Free Trade to prevent the Government of the day

(Heaven knows what that will be!) from returning to Protection when the Anglo French Treaty expires?'

The anxious soul of Cobden was prophetic in its forebodings.

IV

Is it, however, certain that the work of Cobden, and, let us add, of his comrade, Michel Chevalier, is wholly and irreparably destroyed? It seems like it. But for one who is wont to look at the heart of things, appearances are deceptive.

So far as England is concerned, Free Trade is still no more than menaced. It remains in force to the present day. The farmers have obtained Parliamentary grants, relief of rates, and certain indirect benefits not altogether sincere, such as the exclusion of cattle under the pretence of security against disease; but no systematic violation of Free Trade has yet occurred in the United Kingdom. The sugar refiners thought they had succeeded a few years ago in imposing duties on sugar imported from countries which grant bounties to their own manufacturers; but at the last moment Parliament shrank from this violation of principle, however plausible the excuses which could be offered. The greatest danger which threatens Free Trade in England is the plan propounded by some of the 'Imperial Federationists,' under the name of an Imperial Customs Union; but there are very many and important obstacles in the way of a realisation of such plans. We take leave to doubt whether they could assume a practical shape, and still more, assuming that they could be carried into practice, whether so delicate and complicated an organisation could long survive.*

Economic reaction in France, obstinate as it has shown itself to be, has not quite carried us back to the state of things existing before 1860. We do not at this moment prohibit any article in our markets, as a large number were prohibited in the reign of Louis Philippe, and in the early years of the Empire. The sliding-scale for cereals has not been restored, and however high the duties on corn may be, yet they are better than the arbitrary regulation of other days. And so with the *surtaxe de pavillon;* it has had its day. Raw materials, both such as compete with our national products and such as have no rival products in our own country, like wool and cotton, continue to be

---

* The *Statist* for April 18, 1896, prints a series of reports from Australia which illustrate the difficulties of this plan.

free from taxation. It will be remembered
how keen a fight there was on this point,
· after the war of 1870-1, between Thiers and
the Chambers, and how the premier was
compelled to give way. The drawbacks,
with the enormous frauds and loss to the
Treasury which resulted from them, have not
been renewed. It is true that sundry primes
exist in connection with the silk, linen and
hemp manufactures, but that is a comparatively slight evil. In short, though our
actual duties are heavy, they are still, in the
case of a majority of articles, lighter than
those which Cobden and Michel Chevalier
set themselves to modify. Thus the existing tariff, whilst it involves a somewhat
aggravated form of Protection, and a distinct
reaction from the work achieved in 1860, is
far from having carried us all the way back
to the old-fashioned system destroyed by

that famous treaty. There are still some traces of the work of Michel Chevalier and Cobden.

There is ground for the hope that, at no distant period, the economic reaction which has continued with such force during the past fifteen years will give place to a revival of the principles of free exchange, and that France, if not the generality of nations, will return to a belief in Free Trade. It would be wrong to despair; but for all that we must not ignore the strength of the causes which have driven the nations of Europe into Protection. It is quite a recent phenomenon, not anticipated twenty years ago, which sapped the edifice raised in 1860, and discredited it amongst a considerable number of our contemporaries. And this phenomenon was a serious revolution in the domain of agriculture.

If industrial and commercial interests had been alone at stake, it is very probable that the civilised world would have continued to advance in the path opened up for it by Chevalier and Cobden, or at least that it would not have relapsed very far. Up to 1880, moreover, in spite of our calamities, there was no deviation from our Free Trade ideas. It was not until after what has been called the agricultural crisis that the ideas of Free Trade lost ground to a serious extent, and eventually fell into disrepute with many of those who but lately adhered to them.

Now we must not shut our eyes to the fact that it is no mere agricultural crisis which has overtaken Europe, but a complete revolution in agriculture, and in rural property generally. Never since the sixteenth century have men witnessed a revolu-

tion so profound and so rapid. With corn
dropping, in less than twenty years, from
24 or 25 francs for the metric quintal to
11 or 12 francs in bond; with many agricultural products, even of the higher class,
like cheese and butter, subject to a similar
drop; with scarcely a single product of the
farm, eggs and poultry excepted, which has
not been enormously depreciated; it is easy
to understand the changed condition of
those who own the soil and of those who
are tied to it. Of course, it may be said
that this lowering of price must confer a
palpable and definite gain on civilised
countries, in the shape of abundant food
more easily obtained, and that in the few
countries which have clung to Free Trade—
England is to-day the solitary example,
and even England admits certain insincere
modifications — the masses of the popula-

tion are great gainers by paying 11 or 12 francs for a quintal of corn instead of 24 or 25 francs, and from 25 to 50 per cent. less than formerly for meat, butter and other articles of food. Yet it can readily be understood that from this change, as from every sudden and profound change in one of the principal industries, and in the principal industry of all on the continent of Europe, there have resulted a great dislocation of the general economic order, and a period of painful transition.

The revolution in agriculture destroys the value of property, as well as all confidence in the future of that property. In countries like Prussia, where the upper class has not ceased to be territorial, and where it still retains an influence over public affairs, it naturally goes to faddists and charlatans for a remedy in its misfortune; and the same thing occurs in democratic countries, where middle-class or peasant proprietors own the greater part of the soil. It is idle to say that the small proprietor is less affected than the great landlord, because he consumes a large portion of his own productions. He does not consider himself less seriously involved, when he compares the prices of to-day with the prices of the past. He sees the market value of his acre or his hectare diminishing, and his heart is wrung by it; he is too narrow-minded to realise the importance of the indirect compensations which tell in his favour.　-

This revolution in agriculture, then, is the sole cause of the check and the relapse of Free-Trade ideas. It is well to recognise the precise causes of this revolution. It can hardly yet be said that a definite judgment has been formed upon them, and they have received very superficial and ignorant treatment. The phenomenon has been ascribed to some mysterious influence of the scarcity of money, due to the abandonment of silver as a medium of exchange and a legal tender between the chief civilised nations. Others can see nothing but an outcome of foreign competition. The former explanation is absurd; the latter is far too narrow.

The actual cause, wide in its application and far-reaching in its effects of the depreciation of agricultural property all over the world—for the United States are beginning to suffer like ourselves—is the great influence of modern developments, chemical, physical, mechanical, mineral, and even agricultural. In the first place, these developments have produced in the mineral kingdom a number of successful rivals to the productions of the soil. Roscher has observed, very justly, that the human race, in its utilisation of matter for the supply of its needs, began with the animal kingdom, went on to the vegetable, and finally had recourse to the mineral kingdom. A few striking examples may be quoted of this revolution, which is and must continue to be disastrous to property in land. A red dye has been obtained successively from the purple fish, from the madder plant, and then, in our own day, from alizarine, a mineral product   Light has been obtained from suet or fat, then from olive oil, oil of poppies, colza and sesame, but to-day we use petroleum, which is a mineral. Wood has almost given place, for heating purposes, to coal, and has largely given place for building, and for many instruments, to iron. Minerals are put to many new uses. Turf is used as litter, instead of straw; sugar can now be obtained from mineral sub-stances and, a few years ago, the invention of saccharine caused quite a stir; minerals are beginning to be used for tissues, and artificial silks have metal in their composi-tion. There is no reason why minerals should not, ultimately, form a considerable element in the food of man. In a recent work on the 'Theory and Practice of Politi-cal Economy' I quoted a curious toast of M. Berthelot's at a banquet, in 1894, of the Chamber of Chemical Products. The famous chemist broached the fancy that, in, the year 2000, the mineral kingdom would supply mankind with all his food, and that the surface of the earth would be trans-formed into a mere pleasure garden. We are far enough, no doubt, from the realisa-tion of this dream, and it is probable that we shall never completely attain to it; yet every day the developments of chemistry and physics raise up new rivals to the products of agriculture.

Further demonstration is scarcely needed. The progress of electric tramways in North America has sent down the price of horses by one-third or one-half, and has produced a corresponding effect in the price of fodder. It is likely enough that we shall one day be in the same case, though, thanks to our inertness, the change may come less rapidly, and be less complete.

Even the simple developments of farming are in the long run prejudicial to the value of agricultural land. As the result of a more scientific culture, the production of all commodities on a given area is con-siderably increased. Now, since population tends — according to a law which I have often stated*—to increase at a slower rate when a country advances further in civilisation, it follows that the commodities thus produced in greater abundance can only be disposed of by a large diminution of price; and, as a consequence, many farmers are involved in a loss.

The natural outcome of these manifold new developments is that agriculture will have to contract its limits and revise its methods, and many farms less favourably situated, on the hillsides and in poor soil, will have to be abandoned. Capital invested in land is shrinking to a serious extent. Agricultural property shows a general tendency towards uncertain profits and shifting value. It is productive only in skilful hands, but without skill it is unproductive.

* See, for instance, the work above mentioned, vol. iv., second edition.

We can readily understand how disastrous this transition must be for the classes which are bound down to the soil, whether as owners or as farmers. The sufferers are apt to conclude that the mere influx of foreign products suffices to bring about a series of disturbances which, as a matter of fact, are due to far wider and deeper causes. Hence it comes that in almost every country the agricultural classes clamour for protection, when they do not show a preference for other unsound remedies, such as bimetallism.

Will Free Trade eventually win back the support of the rural classes, or triumph over their opposition? Sooner or later it may be so. When the period of transition is at an end, when agricultural property has been consolidated, when land has been acquired on more favourable terms by competent and enterprising men who are wise

enough to use it as an instrument, and
not as an inexhaustible source of constant
revenue; when, moreover, it is recognised
that the chief cause of the falling prices
of agricultural products is not foreign competition, and that these falling prices have
compensating advantages for the mass of
the population, then Protection may once
more lose ground. The tendency of the
towns to predominate over the country,
which is illustrated in every land, and the
steady immigration into the towns, may
contribute towards this revulsion of opinion.
The town populations will realise that it is
hard to have to pay a quarter or a half
as much again for their food as they need
pay. But considerable time must elapse
before the profound revolution which has
taken place in the agricultural world during
the past fifteen years can cease to create

a strong opposition to liberal ideas on economic questions. The recent zeal of the English Government, notwithstanding the enormous preponderance of industrial interests in this country, in allaying the grievances of the farmers by a remission of rates, bears ample witness to the difficulty of turning a deaf ear to their complaints.

Will the ideas of Cobden return to favour more rapidly in the colonies? It has been seen that, from our point of view, Cobden had made a mistake in this direction. I see no reason to regret having been one of the pioneers of the colonial movement in France. The member for Rochdale ignored the tutorial mission of Europe, in the present epoch, in relation to most of the Asiatic nations, and to the scattered and uncivilised tribes of Africa. His conception of the relations between a great civilised nation and the primitive races, unable to work the vast areas which they occupy, is far too narrow. For certain races, and within certain climes, civilisation must be introduced from without; a benevolent and persevering guardianship is necessary to develop it amongst them. Cobden closed his eyes to everything connected with colonisation, except the faults and crimes which have often attended it. He was like those extreme advocates of temperance who oppose even a rational and moderate use of harmless or serviceable liquors, on the ground that they are liable to misuse. Colonisation must be rendered moral, and not absolutely vetoed; it must be purged of barbarous incidents, so far as the nature of man will allow. It is lamentable to see the excesses of Pizarro and Cortez renewed in our own time; but

it is a good thing to extend the civilisation of Europe over the plains of Africa,
and to turn to account the resources of a
continent abandoned to sloth, massacre and
devastation. Nevertheless, the energy with
which Cobden denounced the 'aggressive
character' of his countrymen is to be commended. We can only hope that an enlightened public opinion, without diverting
Englishmen, or any other European nation,
from the noble and beneficent task of
colonisation, will impose on all the founders
of colonial empire more of moderation and
good faith in the accomplishment of their
mission.

In one respect the ideas of Cobden seem
to be making progress in our generation.
The principle of international arbitration,
though we cannot expect that it will completely triumph for some time to come, has,

during the past few years, been put in force
with commendable frequency. Differences
between sundry great nations, of minor importance no doubt, and affecting their self-
esteem rather than their essential interests,
have been smoothed away by this device.
It would be rash to conclude that the system
of arbitration is on the point of being universally accepted, and that it will obviate
every war. At the same time these precedents, however comparatively small the
disputes with which they concern themselves,
should be welcomed as indicating, at any-rate,
a partial advance towards perfection in international relations.

Thus, then, the noble career of Cobden
was fertile in good. It secured for England,
perhaps definitely, the supremacy in commerce which was an indispensable condition
of a full expansion of the power of Great

Britain. More than that, it produced during a quarter of a century, beyond the British frontiers, an abundant harvest for the welfare and moral progress of civilised humanity as a whole. In our own days, the force of his teaching and of his example, though it has been weakened by new times and new circumstances, is not entirely exhausted. This is enough for the glory of Cobden, since few men can boast of having performed a work which endured for a longer period undiminished and without modification.

A JUBILEE OF FREE TRADE AND DEMOCRACY

A JUBILEE OF FREE TRADE AND DEMOCRACY

BY THEODOR BARTH
Member of the German Reichstag

I

IF I were asked what Parliamentary measure, in the history of England during the present century, I considered the most significant, I should answer without a moment's hesitation, 'The abolition of the taxes on corn, which received the royal assent on June 27, 1846'; and to this measure, indeed, I assign not merely a specially economic, but also a political significance of the highest kind.

The democratization of England dates properly from this point of time. It was no doubt initiated by the electoral reform of 1832; but the first great consequence of the democratic movement was the repeal of the aristocratic Corn Laws. And thus it was quite in accordance with political logic that, under the pressure of this momentous event, the old Tory party fell to pieces, and gave place more and more to the modern Toryism of the converted demagogue Disraeli, whilst on the other hand the old Whigs were stirred to their depths, and every Radical tendency made itself conspicuous, compelling the Whigs —sometimes much against their will—to prepare the way for ever-advancing democratic demands. By nothing is this democratic development more clearly shown than by the political career of Gladstone, whom Macaulay hailed, on his first appearance on the political stage, as 'the rising hope of the stern and unbending Tories,' and who, in his old age, was exposed to the grim animosity of the Conservatives as being the most influential leader of political Radicalism.

It is therefore only just and right that the fiftieth anniversary of the day on which the English corn duties were buried should be celebrated as a memorable political Jubilee. Above all, the Cobden Club is naturally disposed to commemorate the event in a festive spirit, seeing that it was founded in memory of the most prominent leader of the Anti-Corn Law League. The club recognises it as its proper task to maintain the traditions of the Manchester school. Yet Cobden established rather a democratic than an economic school. Léon Say spoke very much to the point on this subject, in a lecture which he gave on January 15, 1884, to the Saint Simon Club, on 'State Socialism in England':—'Richard Cobden was, above all things, a thorough democrat, and his followers trusted before everything else that he would establish democracy upon the ruins of the aristocracy, and that he would destroy whatever was left to the great landowners of their feudal privileges.'

The duties on corn were seen to be essentially a monopoly of the great landowners, maintained at the cost of the poorer classes, and as such they were attacked at the outset by the great majority of Cobden's followers. The economic principles by which Cobden was guided in this struggle were naturally of equal weight with that majority. Free Trade commended itself, in the battle against the monopolies of the territorial aristocracy, as the most practical political weapon; and men like Cobden and Bright—in whose minds the axioms of Free Trade shaped themselves into guiding principles for their combined attempt to simplify the economic life of the nation—were also naturally the best fitted to be leaders in this movement. These men, furthermore, had a clear conception of the fundamental connection between the intervention of the State in the fiscal domain, by exerting an influence upon the natural rise and fall of prices, and the intervention of the State in other economic domains, by influencing the rate of production. Cobden and Bright, therefore, were both decided opponents of State Socialism.

But the political school which they founded concerned itself much more closely with the struggle against the privileges of the land-owning aristocracy. This struggle has never ceased in England since the abolition of the Corn Laws, and a considerable section of the Manchester school has always regarded it as the special legacy of Cobden. The chief representative of this tendency, up to the disruption of Mr Gladstone's party, was Mr Joseph Chamberlain, now Colonial Secretary in the Cabinet of Lord Salisbury. He did not even recoil from experiments in State Socialism, when it seemed worth while, to weaken the power of the aristocratic landowners ; and in particular he contended energetically for the limitation of free ownership of land and estates.

This schism in the old historical Manchester school between the State-Socialist Radicals and the Individualist Liberals became especially acute in the year 1883, on the occasion of the admission of the French Radical Clémencean as an honorary member of the Cobden Club. His admission induced a few prominent Liberal economists — amongst them being Mr Goschen, the future First Lord of the Admiralty—to resign their

membership. The significance of this occurrence was further emphasised by the
characteristic bluntness with which Mr
Chamberlain, at the Cobden Club banquet
held shortly afterwards, was at pains to
ascribe the resignation of these members to
antagonism on matters of principles.

These few indications should be quite
enough to justify the title of the present
essay. It concerns itself with the commemoration of the abolition of the Corn Laws,
not merely as a jubilee of Free Trade, but
also as a jubilee of democracy. At the
same time, it is concerned with the commemoration of a political event which has
exercised the greatest influence, far beyond
the borders of Great Britain, upon the
economic institutions of other lands, and
upon the commercial relations of different
countries.

II

With the collapse of the corn duties, the victory of Free Trade in England was completed. The repeal of the Navigation Acts followed, with Mr Gladstone's reforms, in and after 1853, in matters of Customs and Excise, and finally, in 1860, the Commercial Treaty between England and France was concluded. This was the beginning of an era of international commercial negotiations which in a short time united almost the whole of Europe with a network of treaties. It seemed at that time as if the Free Trade movement would continue without a check, and extend its victories throughout the world.

Nobody could have imagined that by the close of the decade ending with 1879 an exceptionally strong reaction against the

Free Trade movement would have set in. And no man can be held more responsible for this reaction than Prince Bismarck.

In Germany itself, and especially in Prussia, the policy of Free Trade appeared to be thoroughly established. Long before the maxims of Free Trade had permeated England, the Prussian Customs reform of 1818 had been enacted. The intelligence of the Prussian statesmen of that day, and their freedom from prejudice in matters of fiscal policy, cannot be better illustrated than by the preliminary report of January 14, 1817, wherein a plan of Customs legislation was put forward, and by the report of the Parliamentary Commission, which, under the presidency of Wilhelm von Humboldt, had laid down the lines of an inquiry. Thus, for instance, we find it stated in the per-liminary report of 1817 :—'The most pro-

lific source of well-being is trade. Just as
in our own country, in order to advance
our prosperity, the hindrances to free sale
and competition are removed, so it is un-
doubtedly for the welfare of the nation and
a matter of prudence to grant systematic
Free Trade in our intercourse with foreign
nations.'

This was such an advanced point of
view, for the time in which it was written,
that, in the year 1820, the City of London,
in a petition to the House of Commons,
referred to the Prussian Customs reform as
an example worthy of imitation. 'A policy
based upon such principles,' the petition
.declared, 'would render the commerce of
the world an interchange of mutual advantages.' And William Huskinson, in 1827,
referring to the Prussian Customs legislation of 1818, said plainly in the House

of Commons that he hoped the time would soon arrive when Englishmen would be able to congratulate themselves on a similar tariff.

The same clear-sightedness and the same impartial judgment led other Prussian statesmen, in the thirtieth year of the century, to create the Customs Union. This Prussian policy of Free Trade was, in the first half of the century, almost exclusively due to the insight of Prussian officials. It is impossible to speak of any popular party which supported this policy. Not until the year 1850 was Free Trade in any sense popular. Such men as Schulze-Delitsch, Prince-Smith, Faucher, Otto Michaelis, Karl Braun, and many other leading publicists, laboured in speech and writing to create a public opinion; and in 1858 the German Free Trade party forged for itself, in the

Annual Congress of National Economy, an instrument which for two decades exercised a considerable influence on the development of economic and commercial policy. The enlightened Prussian ministers were effectively aided in their efforts to advance Free Trade by the movement finding a fulcrum in the Congress of Economy; and when in 1860 the Franco-Prussian Treaty of Commerce was concluded, it appeared as though Germany would very soon become a radically Free Trade country.

Amongst the Prusso - German statesmen whose insight and practical skill were at that time especially combined for the furthering of Free Trade, the most conspicuous, and for a long while the most successful, was Rudolf Delbrück, who, on the founding of the German Empire, acted as Bismarck's right hand in all matters of commercial and economic policy. Prince Bismark himself at that time seriously entertained the question of a complete abandonment of prohibitory duties, simultaneously with the more distinct maintenance of taxes for revenue. In no quarter was there yet any noteworthy reaction in favour of prohibitory duties, even in the ranks of the great landlords. On the contrary, the landed interest, which at that time considered it quite impracticable ever again to lay a duty on corn, was almost completely and radically Free Trade.

Everything, however, was changed from the end of the seventies. In 1876, Delbrück had fallen away. He had soon recognised that a change of system was approaching.

Under the influence of the economic depression which declared itself in Germany as elsewhere, following upon the crisis of 1873 and endured for twelve months, protectionist demands had gathered strength, first of all in the iron and textile industries. But this industral Protectionism would not have succeeded in breaking down the long-established principles of Free Trade if a combination had not been effected between industrial and agrarian protectionists. Prince Bismarck soon recognised that this combination was necessary in order to effect a fundamental change of the existing policy of taxation and commerce. Careful consideration of a purely political kind made it, however, seem at that time desirable to link his fortunes with those of the Liberal parties, which were the most powerful representatives of the Free Trade policy. When, therefore, in the year 1878, the attempt on the life of the aged Kaiser Wilhelm created a favourable opportunity for reactionary legislation of every kind, the then omnipotent Chancellor went out of his way to effect a diversion towards a system of prohibitory duties. The tariff of 1879 thus came into operation, the significance of which is to be looked for, not so much in the increase of a large number of duties, as in the combination of industrial and agricultural Protective duties. The new duties on wood, cattle and corn, and other products of the land, were still only of a specific character—the corn tax, for instance, was one mark for two hundredweight; but the pregnant question as to subjecting the most important articles of the food of the people to a system of prohibitive duties was involved in this step, and no great foresight was needed to perceive that the tariff would not long continue at this *minimum* rate. As early as 1885 an increase of duties took effect on wheat and rye, from one to three marks for the two hundredweight; and in the year 1887 a further increase to five marks. Agricultural Protection had already made a great advance, and it was not restricted to the operations of the duties. Particular modes of agricultural production, as the distilling of brandy and the manufacture of sugar, were stimulated in all kinds of ways by a highly artificial system of Parliamentary aids. And finally there were added in Prussia still further reliefs for the great landlords in the domain of direct taxation, especially through the remission of the ground tax payable to the State. In brief, the whole system of taxation, of economics and of commercial industry in Germany was made subservient, in the course of a few years, to the interests of the great landlords.

This radically modified economic policy was naturally not without influence on the

general political development of the Empire.
Reaction overtook every phase of the
national life. The chief representatives of
the great landlord's interests : the Prussian
Kleinadel, or Junkers, eagerly promoted this
revolution, in order to enlarge their own
authority. They could not lose by it,
whether in an economic or in a political
sense, so long as all legislation was arranged
to suit the land-owning aristocracy, and, as
they had the support of the omnipotent
Prince Bismarck, they could nurse the most
daring hopes.

Early in the year 1890 Prince Bismarck
was suddenly released from office, and a
general succeeded to his position as imperial Chancellor, who, coming from the
Conservative party, presently proved himself
to be an independent statesman, for whom
the interests of the people, as a whole, were

alone imperative. Count Caprivi declined
to place himself at the service of the land-
owning interest exclusively; his policy inclined much more to a resumption of the
deserted path of commercial treaties; and
it was his pleasure not only to conclude
new treaties with Austria - Hungary, Italy,
Belgium, Roumania and Switzerland, but
also, after a short time, to induce Russia
also to conclude a treaty, though Germany
had never hitherto been able to concert a
tariff agreement with that empire. The
open breach thus made in Prince Bismarck's
prohibitory agrarian tariff—which displayed
itself, amongst other ways, in an abatement
of the German wheat duty from five to three
and a-half marks for the two hundredweight—
was for the Prussian Junkers an ample pre-
text for attacking the Conservative statesman
—who would not regard the interests of the

great landlords as the only ones worthy of consideration more bitterly than Sir Robert Peel had been opposed, on account of the abolition of the Corn Laws, by his former friends the Tories. To the open enmity of these Prussian Junkers. and to their private intrigues, Count Caprivi was finally sacrificed. But the prohibitive agrarian policy had received a heavy blow from the conclusion of Count Caprivi's treaties of commerce. It appears, indeed, as if the height of Protectionist reaction had been reached at the beginning of this new era of commercial treaties throughout the world.

III

Protection is a contagious epidemic amongst the nations. Above all, when a great State with traditions of Free Trade suddenly relapses into a system of prohibitory duties, there is in the mere fact of this inconsistency an inducement for other States to imitate it. The forces of Protectionism are wont to disturb capital with such reactionary effects that they come to possess an *argumentum ad hominem* which, at any rate for the majority of men who are influenced by foreign precedents, is seldom without constraining force. With the change of system adopted by Germany in 1879, came also the additional fact that it was effected by the most influential statesman in the world, Prince Bismarck, whose prestige, rested in the opinion of all men, upon this most important foundation: that his material policy was the outcome of an altogether exceptional political prudence. When such a man established a prohibitory tariff for Germany, it was held that he must know what he was about, and that, consequently, men would be dealing wisely in other countries by putting the same remedy into operation. It is not in my opinion open to the slightest doubt that such a consideration had in no slight degree tended to set to a lively measure the general movement toward Protective tariff.

Accordingly we find that in the eighties, in all European countries except England, was a continually increasing disposition to protect the national industries from foreign competition by raising the import duties. The same phenomenon occurred, at the same time, in the United States of America, and even in Australia. In Germany, France, and the United States—the three most important countries after England for agri-. cultural industry—the Protectionist reaction was especially vigorous. It is associated with the names of Bismarck, Méline and M'Kinley, but by far the most important promoter of the international movement was the German Chancellor.

It is characteristic that this development was also accompanied by many Tariff wars. I will only mention the Tariff wars between Austria and Roumania, France and Italy, France and Switzerland. Caprivi's policy of commercial treaties exercised a moderating influence in regard to the tendency towards a Customs war. The termination of the Tariff war between France and Switzerland is conspicuous for having checked the reactionary mood which immediately ensued in France after the abrogation of the treaty of commerce between Russia and Germany.

England may take credit to herself for having stood fast by the standard of Free

Trade during the high tide of prohibitory duties in the eighties. In England also there was, for a considerable time, a talk of ' Fair Trade.' Protectionists in disguise sought to bring into favour a plan of Free Trade with Reciprocity, and thus to sap the foundations of Free Trade ; but the attempt failed before the common sense of English-men, and especially before the ever-in-creasing strength of the political position of the working men. Through this steady adhesion to Free Trade, England has ex-tended her economic development on sound lines.

That the results of this Free Trade policy, in spite of all transitory crises, have been satisfactory—in the most important respects and in the long run—needs no particular proof. It is only necessary to bear in mind that the trade of Great Britain with other countries is four times as large to-day as it was in 1846; and, indeed, the value of the increase in gold is seen to be much more considerable if the weight of the merchandise is calculated. Not unconnected with that is the fact that in the past half century the number of cases of outdoor relief has steadily decreased, in spite of the large increase of the population. Finally, a glance at the revenue returns for last year shows how it stands with the financial resources of the country. The financial year ending with March 31, 1896, shows, as compared with the previous year, an increase of £7,290,000. In this increase Customs, Excise, the Death Duties, the Income Tax, and the Posts and Telegraphs bear their part; and hence it appears that not only property and income, but also the consumption of the people are notably increasing.

The astounding development of prosperity to which Great Britain is able to point since the abolition of the Corn Laws cannot, of course, be exclusively traced to the adoption of Free Trade; but in a very large measure, at all events, Free Trade has contributed to this development. What weighs in the scale before everything else is the circumstance that no section of the English population has advanced more to the front, since the introduction of Free Trade, than the working men. The advance has been remarkable in two senses, first, by a notable rise in wages, and next by a still more significant adjustment of prices for the necessaries of life. For food in particular, and above all for bread, the English labourer has to devote less out of his earnings to-day than in the times before the abolition of the corn duties, when he had a much smaller rate of wages to count upon, so that in those days there was very little to be said for the chance of setting meat on the workman's table.

IV

That every kind of Protection must be essentially injurious to the working man is, for intelligible reasons, eagerly contested by the friends of prohibition. The tendency of all technical improvements, of all perfections in the conditions of trade, of all inventions, by means of which labour is saved, is insensibly to improve the economic position of the labourers themselves, through the cheapening of the products of labour. It is clear on the face of it that a workman whose actual wages do not fall, but on the contrary increase, as they are shown to have done in the last half century, must profit by every fall in the cost of his food. The measure in which this improvement in the condition of the English working man has been continuously effected is shown by Mr W. Little in his report to the Labour Commission in 1894. According to him, a full-grown male labourer required each week for flour, butter, cheese, tea and sugar :—

In 1860-67,	.	.	.	.	.	.	4s. 2d.
In 1868-75,	.	.	.	.	.	.	4s.
In 1876-83,	.	.	.	.	.	.	3s.
In 1884-91,	.	.	.	.	.	.	2s. 8d.
In 1892-94,	.	.	.	.	.	.	2s. 5d.

Thus in the last three decades the cost of the necessaries of life has been diminished by forty per cent. The many effective improvements of the economic process, as illustrated in every department of industrial life, have in this way brought immediate and very great advantage to the wage-earning class.

The Protectionists are at pains to transfer the credit for the fortunate condition at which Labour has arrived to the other two factors of production, Capital and Rent. Whilst legislation, by prohibitory duties and other Protectionist measures, labours to raise the price of the products of labour, it compels the labourer, through the consequent increase in the cost of the necessaries of life, to give a greater part of his wages in order to obtain what is necessary for his subsistence. This manifest injury could only be compensated by an adequate increase of wages; but that does not come to pass, for indeed it would once more paralyse the operation of Protectionist measures. As a matter of fact, therefore, every artificial increase of price in any of the productions of labour is evidently prejudicial to the interests of labour, and an advantage to the interests of capital, whether industrial capital or capital invested in land.

In this unjust partisanship of Protectionist legislation in favour of the capitalists and against the working men, there is a serious reproach which applies to any kind of Protectionist law. The more Protection aims at improving the condition of the landowners, the more injurious it is; for agricultural protection inevitably succeeds in raising the price of the necessaries of existence—and of bread in particular whereby the landowner is in a position to draw a higher rent from his tenant.

To what an enormous injury of the labourer's position we may be directly brought by this Protection of agriculture may be judged from the fact that the artificial raising of the price of flour, which has been effected by the actual prohibitive duty in Germany of 35 marks per ton on wheat and rye, represents an annual burden upon German labour of at least 150 million marks. And this sum is only a part of that monstrous contribution which German labourers have to pay every year to the great landowners and capitalists who profit by Protection.

What harmony is there between such palpably unjust legislation and the action of the State attested by the excellent laws for the compulsory insurance of working men? There is, in fact, no social system which has been so beneficial to the condition of the workmen as the policy which had its effect in the abolition of the Protectionist laws. Amongst us in Germany the workmen understand this very well; and the Social Democrats also, much as they clamour in theory for the regulation by State intervention of the whole life of the community, have always shown a bold front against the Protectionist invasions of the law. Social democracy in Germany is Free Trade to the last man. That is always the case where labour has learned to recognise its true interests.

But even in regard to the interests of capital, the Protectionist partisanship of the law has in no way resulted in the benefits which were hoped for. The purpose was to raise prices artifically, by means of prohibitive duties, in the home markets; the effect of such prohibitive duties must everywhere be an artificial stimulation of production — on the one side, an artificial multiplication of the Protected article, and on the other side, within the particular region of the duties, a relative diminishing of consumption in respect of these Protected articles, as a consequence of the artificial rise of prices brought about through the duties. In the same proportion as these two operations have taken place, in all the countries which have cut themselves off from one another by constantly rising prohibitive duties, over-production of necessity made itself apparent in the markets of the world; and this over-production has naturally led again to a lowering of price, which, under the simultaneous occurrence of violent crises, has in many ways paralysed the operation of the duties. From this point of view also, Protection appears to be a most hazardous divagation of the law.

V

One naturally asks oneself how it can possibly have happened that Protectionism, revived in our generation, has won such an influence in spite of the considerations above-mentioned. The prohibitive policy stands in most absurd contrast with the assiduous efforts which men make, aided by the utmost technical skill and often with vast expenditure of capital, to remove the obstacles which Nature has set in the way of commerce. How is it possible that the same authorities by whose initiation dividing mountains are pierced, and all countries of the world are joined together with constantly increasing and effectual links of commerce, should put the wits of man to such bad use as to set artificial limits to the commercial exchanges of different nations, in the form of prohibitive legislation? This is a logical contradiction, which indeed is not in any way a rarity in political life, but which at the same time stands in need of special explanation.

L

Such an explanation is not very difficult to find. In plain terms, the disturbance of all the economic relations between different countries, which has followed upon the nineteenth-century revolution amongst the various articles of commerce, has caused a legislative reaction, opposing itself to the manifestations of this revolution. Men feel themselves constrained, by the consequences of this change of conditions, which they have themselves brought about: they would like only to enjoy the advantages of the inflation of trade, to compete themselves without suffering the competition of others. It is especially difficult in the economic domain to make the mass of mankind understand that there is no light without a shadow, and that the stronger the light the darker must the shadow be; and thus it is easy to see that, when all those whom the shoe pinches unite together and urge the law-givers to protect them from foreign competitors, those who make the laws become weak, and set up a system of Protection. Certainly such manifestations of reaction are frequently observed in the transitional periods of economic history. Men have not yet established themselves under the new conditions, and they are in the meanwhile experimenting with all sorts of legislative remedies.

It may safely be said that this protectionist reaction will not long continue. Yet when a single nation, as is the case with England, has not lost her head in such a reactionary period, she may well be proud of the fact. Nor does it seem very likely that England will suffer a relapse into Protection, since the Protectionist fever has manifestly declined in other lands. No politician, and least of all a Conservative, can seriously think to-day of putting prohibitive duties on the necessary food of the people. Lord Salisbury not long since candidly recognised the fact; and if an English government like the present one, which is so closely bound up with the interests of the great landlords, cannot think of such a thing, Who will ever be strong enough in England to undo the work of Cobden and Peel? The democratic spirit has become too strong in England for any man to risk such a cynical violation of the interests of the great masses of the people.

It is indeed not merely a Jubilee of Free Trade, but also a Jubilee of Democracy.

THE COBDEN CLUB AND THE FIFTIETH ANNIVERSARY OF THE REPEAL OF THE CORN LAWS

THE COBDEN CLUB AND THE FIFTIETH ANNIVERSARY OF THE REPEAL OF THE CORN LAWS

BY THE RIGHT HON. LEONARD H. COURTNEY, M.P.

[THE address of the Right Hon. Leonard H. Courtney, M.P., in proposing the toast of 'The Cobden Club and the Fiftieth Anniversary of the Repeal of the Corn Laws,' in his place as Chairman of the Corn Law Repeal Jubilee Dinner given by the Cobden Club, on the 27th of June 1896, at the Ship Hotel, Greenwich.]

We are assembled to-day not merely to keep up the sequence of the banquets of this club, but to celebrate the fiftieth anniversary of the acceptance, in its fullest form, of Free Trade within this realm.

We are here to-day to express our belief in the wisdom of our fathers in what they did so long back, to express our faith in their principles now, and to pledge ourselves, as long as any strength and life is left in us, to maintain those principles in the future. The fifty years that have passed have only proved the wisdom of what was then done.

It is indeed customary, my lords and gentlemen, to give you comparative figures of the condition of countries which are under the respective principles of Free Trade and Protection. I do not repeat them now because I believe they are often illusory, and to my mind at least they have never been convincing. The circumstances of nations so differ from one another that it is impossible to bring these crowded masses of figures into comparison, and to say that, because you will discover such and such a state of circumstances in one country and such and such a state of circumstances in another, these consequences are to be attributed to the adoption of one or the other theory of fiscal legislation. We may confess that a country may be prosperous although it has adopted a Protective *régime.* It is prosperous not because of Protection, but in spite of it. We may also confess— although perhaps this is a harder statement to accept — we may also confess that the population and commerce of a country may dwindle though that country has adopted Free Trade. I do not know whether that will at once commend itself to all of you, but upon a little reflection you will perceive that it must be true. In our own country certain portions, under our Free Trade *régime*—I will not say in consequence of it — have diminished their population, and have also suffered a diminution in their commercial transactions; and what is possible of a part of this country in respect of the whole, may be possible of this country also in respect of the rest of the world. The time may be coming when, although we have adopted and shall continue to maintain the principles of Free Trade, our position may not be unchanged, our population may have to undergo a decline, our commercial position in the world may indicate some falling off. But when that happens, if it is to happen, it will not be in consequence of Free Trade. Free Trade is what we shall rely upon upon to break the fall—to put off what may be the inevitable change.

No; instead of inviting you to compare

nation with nation, I would ask you rather to consider the position of each nation by itself. Consider our own country. As I have said, we are here to testify to our faith. Looking back these fifty years, I think I may say for everyone here and for the great army of martyrs outside, that we have watched with unwavering faith the course of that history. Never for one moment in the whole period have we who have passed through it—or younger ones who can look back upon it—never can we detect a position in which we should not have been worse off if Protection should have been maintained, and in which we should not be worse off if we reverted to Protection now.

Fasten your mind upon any point of the history of the country. Conceive for a moment such a fatality—it is only conceivable in hypothesis—consider the adoption of a Protective *régime*, and you will see from that moment that the progress of the nation is checked, expansion is limited, its movement is dwarfed, its industry is crippled, the reward of its labours is diminished. This we say of ourselves, and when we look abroad and see other countries which have prospered—in spite of false principles of legislation as we believe—we can still bear witness to our creed by saying that if Germany has developed as it has, it would have developed still more if instead of Protection it had adopted Free Trade.

France has shown under great trials that marvellous vitality which still retains her rank among nations, but if France and French legislation had been wise enough to follow what we thought would be adopted

—Free Trade in that country—France would have been still more vital, still more active, and still more have demonstrated her place in the world.

And so of the United States. I believe some of us who look at it are accustomed to contemplate with feelings of peril what would happen if the United States would adopt Free Trade. I cherish for my part no such fears. I believe that if to-morrow Free Trade were adopted in the United States we should be able to exult in the great expansion of the Republic across the Atlantic; but we should be able at the same time to reflect that that expansion would produce an increased well-being among ourselves.

What is true of this and other countries is true of our colonies. There is not a single colony, as far as I know, which has adopted Protective principles without adopting them to its hurt. I know that ingenious people have conceived conditions under which new communities may be excused for adopting Protection. It is an ingenious hypothesis. When you look at the fact of any community which can be submitted to you no support is found for that hypothesis. It requires no artifical help to develop the industrial resources of a community if the natural circumstances of that community are favourable to that development.

And here we have, strange to say, the strongest testimony of proof from the United States themselves. The United States form a continent. They are a great area; they cover a great area, with a mighty people, a diversified climate, diversified soil, conditions of production varying

to the highest degree, industries flourish-
ing in the older States, and mining communities in some of the younger. There,
you would say, artifical aids to develop
industry were wanted. But without any
assistance from legislation there have sprung
up in the South and West—wherever the
opportunity offered—there have sprung up
industrial communities of all kinds, industrial activities of all variety. Especially
since the regeneration of the South, the
South has become a manufacturing region
like the North, although the South to the
North is as far removed in circumstances
and conditions as are the antipodean colonies
from ourselves. Without any aid of tariff
or bounty, owing to national circumstances
alone and entirely, there have sprung up these
industries in the South to rival, and in some
cases to outrun, the industries of the North.

Looking, therefore, at ourselves, looking at foreign countries, looking at the colonies, the records of past years warrant us in holding fast by the belief in which we have been bred and in which we live. We were Free Traders yesterday; we are Free Traders to-day; we mean to be Free Traders for ever.

Yet we have to confess that the hopes of those who preceded us fifty years ago have not been realised. It has been a great disappointment of the expectations then fondly entertained. Some of them were obviously too sanguine, too little founded upon a knowledge of human nature and human history.

I recall sometimes a prophecy which was made by one of the most eloquent advocates of the Repeal of the Corn Laws, in which he is reported to have said that

'after the Corn Laws had been repealed
for a few years the poor-houses of our
land would become uninhabited barracks,
and would soon become the monuments of
history like the desolate castles of the
Plantagenets and Tudors.' Our workhouses
have not fallen into decay. They are still
too full; they are still wanted. We have
abolished the Corn Laws, established Free
Trade, but half a century has not abolished
pauperism. But could it, as long as human
nature contains any of its vicious elements;
as long as men are improvident; as long
as life is thriftless and the future is allowed
to take care of itself?

No Repeal of the Corn Laws or anything will bring about that consummation for
which we hope, but there are more moderate
expectations which might have been fulfilled.
Mr Cobden, our great, our honoured chief,

M

made a tour of Europe after the Repeal of the Corn Laws. He was *fêted* in public assemblies, he was also the guest of royalty, he was everywhere recognised as the hero who had won, after a long and arduous fight with the strongest forces in the most Conservative country in Europe. He would surely be justified in thinking that in a few years the triumph which he had achieved, for which he was acclaimed, would be perfected by its acceptance throughout Europe. But that has not been. Why has it not been? We must confess the disappointment. We ought in some way or other to be able to understand why this disappointment has happened.

For my own part, when I look back at the history of the Repeal of the Corn Laws among ourselves, I am not so much surprised at the slowness of the progress of Free

Trade among other nations. We glory in the fact; we cannot be proud of the way in which that fact was accomplished. Yesterday we tendered our congratulations to our old friend Mr Villiers. But pray consider what our friend Mr Villiers had to go through. What weary years, what hopeless years of work he had to undergo! A man of family and fashion, it was to his infinite honour that he took up the cause of the Repeal of the Corn Laws. The youngest man in the House of Commons to-day, who sits upon its backest benches, who is regarded as the greatest of bores, as the most unpractical of men, may take hope in thinking that he may be occupying the position which Mr Villiers occupied sixty years since, and that he has a future to avenge him as Mr Villiers has been avenged by his past during the last half century. When Mr Villiers began, we had as Prime Minister a man of great ability, Lord Melbourne. Lord Melbourne said he had heard of many mad things in his life, but he never heard of anything madder than the notion of repealing the Corn Laws. Lord Melbourne was a man of ability in my judgment. Although perhaps it is hazardous, I would say he was up to the level of Prime Ministers.

But if you think that too strong, pass on to consider Sir Robert Peel. Sir Robert Peel was up to the level and beyond it, and Sir Robert Peel went on floundering with his sliding scale. Sir Robert Peel was not alone. Lord John Russell had his 8s. fixed duty. That is what you call statesmanship. These men went on in their beliefs, and Sir Robert Peel came in at the head of a great majority—supported by the common sense of the nation. Do not blink these unpleasant truths. It was not until we were face to face with famine and death, following upon famine and pestilence —it was not until these things happened that Sir Robert Peel felt himself bound to abandon all his arguments and open the ports to the corn which should come to feed the starving. If we — our ancestors were at least as wise as we are—if our ancestors were so slow to receive what we believe to be almost self-evident truths, can we find fault, can we be astonished if other nations are slow to receive them?

Nay, I go from the past generation to the present. I ask myself why it is that the progress of Free Trade has been so slow in spite of our example. I am inclined sometimes to look at home. I have often read of a great personage of to-day making speeches and saying we have adopted Free Trade, and we have nothing to bargain with, and how can we persuade other countries to be Free Traders. And when I have read those remarks I have been sometimes tempted to say—always to myself—' Lord Salisbury, you want other nations to believe in Free Trade, begin by believing in it yourself.'

But let us put some questions nearer home. Have the language and conduct of ourselves been always free from ambiguity? Are there any within our cause who have sustained the belief—the fallacious belief of others—that the adoption of Free Trade is a loss? We have chaffered and bargained, as though it were a sacrifice to adopt Free Trade and we should make sacrifice to induce others to make sacrifice. Let our action be clearer and our language be freer. No chaffering, but a fervent faith in the faith as we have believed it, as we have accepted it, and then I think we may hope that we shall not be discouraged; we may hope for a more rapid advancement in the future of what we have to confess has been so tardily advanced in the past. We may at least wait. We are not going to change one iota. Not one footstep will we withdraw from the position we entertain, but we may wait in the fullness of faith which overcomes all obstacles: in the fullness of faith the truth will in time be manifest.

Yes, we will wait, but we must not sleep. The truth is being sown abroad, I am glad to know, in all lands, but the tares are being sown also. The enemy is very vigilant, very active; and private interests, class interests, trade interests, monopolies of commerce, the glamour of assumed patriotism —all these are worked upon in turn so as to lead us astray.

Well, we can meet our enemies. I hope we can meet all opponents, but those against whom I specially warn you are the enemies who appear under the guise of friends. Free Trade is never so much in peril as from those who come saying, 'We are Free Traders, but—' If they were to complete that sentence truly—I do not mean to say they are consciously false, but if they went to the bottom of their thoughts and turned themselves inside out and came out with the truth, they would say, 'We are Free Traders, but we are not.' 'We are Free Traders, but—but in order to procure Free Trade amongst other nations it is necessary to establish some duties which we shall be able in time to remit. Reciprocity is the way to establish Free Trade.'

That is all very old history. The way in which men come to you to-day, repeat-

ing these sentiments which they have dis-
covered, is one of the surprises of experience.
It is quite old history. Sir Robert Peel
tried that dodge and failed, and the moment
you set up duties in order, as you say, to
take them away when you can get other
countries to consent to take them away,
from that moment you set up duties in
other countries also. You establish from that
moment antagonism. From that moment
you have new difficulties to fight and new
difficulties to overcome. I read—or rather
I had read to me—during the last few
days observations in an Austrian journal
with reference to the latest suggestion of
imperial Free Trade. The writer said, 'It
will not be adopted in Great Britain now,
but it may be in the future, and it behoves
us to take care and take steps to protect
ourselves against contingencies that may

happen.' That is the way you are going to set up Free Trade—putting tariffs up to pull them down.

But can our country make itself dependent upon the supplies of necessaries from other countries? Must we not be bound to find within ourselves the means for sustaining our own existence?

This is one of those things which deceive the very elect. And I want to put it in the broadest way, the most emphatic form I can, when I declare for myself that the more I can make this nation dependent upon other people the more I would do it. If I could so inextricably twine up and twist together the dealings of ourselves and France, ourselves and the United States, ourselves and Germany, that it would be impossible for human ingenuity or human malice to conceive of the rending of the union, I would.

And why not? After all, the world has lasted many thousands of years. The geologists are going on increasing the thousands. Figures we were contented with as boys we are obliged to discard to-day. It is not a long way back since the elements of this United Kingdom were separated one from another, and for an Englishman to hate a Scot, and for a Scot to hate an Englishman was the natural order of events. But happily now we are so tied together that as it would be impossible to do without grouse shooting or deer forests, it is idle to conceive of England or Scotland ever being separated. I hope we may look forward to a future when all the component parts of the United Kingdom are joined together in a union which cannot admit of the possibility of disunion. So we may look forward to the time — we have some warrant in expecting it now—when at least the United States and ourselves may be so knit and tied together in commercial interests as well as in the natural union of a kindred tongue, kindred literature, and for a long time of a common history, that it shall be absolutely impossible to conceive of the separation of the two countries.

But I come to yet another, the very latest form of action suggested in the interests of Free Trade. It is that this kingdom of ours and its colonies shall unite together with perfect Free Trade among themselves and with perfect exclusion of the rest of the world.

That is the latest suggestion which we have had for promoting Free Trade. Well now, at one time this United Kingdom did have Free Trade amongst its component parts and exclusion as far as was possible of the rest of the world. We gave preference to our own corn. We gave preference to the silks of Spitalfields. We gave preference to the ribbons of Coventry, and to all sorts of minor manufactures, and we endeavoured to make ourselves self-contained and self-sustained; but we came more than fifty years ago to the conclusion that that was a mistake. Is there any reason for believing that the policy which was a mistake within the United Kingdom could be other than a mistake within the United Empire? Could we expect as possible a permanent arrangement reproducing the characteristics of internal Free Trade and external Protection?

Let the Colonies understand this—if they are at all tempted to entertain it—that if it were entered upon for one moment it would be entered upon with the intention of breaking it down. If we consented to establish this Zollverein it would be for the purpose of putting an end to it as soon as possible after it was accomplished. That would depreciate for our part the merits of the transaction. If we could be persuaded to entertain it, it would be for the purpose of putting an end to it. Could we entertain it?

I am disposed to have the most open mind towards all suggestions. Mr Cobden had a mind which was free to receive the thoughts and the ideas of all men and of all nations. It will be hard to characterise him in any one sentence, but I think this might be said of him without hesitation : that he had no hostile tariff of prejudice to exclude ideas that came from others. He was a Free Trader in the matter of ideas as much as in the matter of commodities, and I am not sure—I tread possibly over suppressed fires—that the Cobden Club has always shown that supreme openness of mind of its patron saint, and shown itself ready to entertain suggestions, however apparently heterodox, coming from quarters however apparently unfruitful of good.

Let us look the matter in the face. I am not prepared to say — I hope I shall not lose my reputation by the confession —that under no circumstances could I conceive a Free Trader entering into a Zollverein. If all the world except two nations were in one Zollverein, it would be a great temptation to one of the two excluded to enter into that union. It would not necessarily be for its benefit. That would depend upon a comparison of its trade with the other excluded nation and the rest of the world. But I can conceive of circumstances under which it would be even proper and right, in the promotion of industry, for an excluded nation to submit to that choice. That is very fanciful. I put another suggestion more practicable. If, instead of the wisdom that governs the American Republic, there had been allowed to grow up, between its component commonwealths, barriers of tariff—if instead of its being part of a constitution with no duty levied on the transit of goods from one state to another and perfect freedom allowed, the United States had experienced a commonwealth of different and hostile tariffs, instead of one which endeavoured to follow Free Frade, it would be a great temptation to one commonwealth to enter into a Zollverein for the abolition of internal duties within all that vast continent. I do not say it would not be to the benefit of the country to do it. If I were a member of one of the Australian colonies, and being a strong Free Trader myself, I think I might consent to enter into a union with all the other Australian colonies, consenting for a time to a tariff around the continent, always with the intention of using my energies within the union to get rid of those duties as soon as I could.

Admitting these possibilities, What is the verdict to which you must come in looking at the suggestion of this imperial Zollverein? Look at it in a part of England, or the United Kingdom, or the Colonies. In the first place, Is it in the interests of Free Trade or not that it is propounded? Those who first moot the suggestion say it is because you cannot get Free Trade advanced any other way, and they are trying this way of getting it promoted. I put a little question just to see how far it will hold good.

N

There is nothing in the notion of uniting together the Empire in one Zollverein, but if it is only to promote Free Trade the bigger the Zollverein the better. What do you say to making it a Zollverein not merely of the dependencies of the British Crown, but of all English speaking communities, asking the United States to join it? Well, they won't. Ask them, then, to join it, and what would be the effect upon those Australian colonies or those other colonies which are now being asked to join it? If as Free Traders we suggested that the United States should come in, they (the Colonies) would say, 'This is not our notion. We, if we are going into it, are going in as Protectionists, and to admit a rival like the United States would upset the transaction.' Is it Free Trade? Is it Protection? The truth is, it is double-faced. On one side it presents the aspect of Free Trade, and on the other side the aspect of Protective duties.

It is a detail that this scheme has been put before us as a scheme of bringing three hundred millions of people within a Free Trade agreement. Three hundred millions of people! I was surprised to find that a man of the stubborn and independent intelligence of the Chancellor of the Exchequer, Sir Michael Hicks-Beach, repeated those unthinking figures the other day. Three hundred millions of people! That includes all the inhabitants of British India. They are Free Traders already. Nine-tenths of the three hundred millions are in the Zollverein, and it is the other tenth you are talking about, instead of these three hundred millions you parade across the sea.

Now, let us look at the thing itself. To the people of Great Britain, What does it suggest? The suggestion is that you are to have additional duties on corn, wool, sugar, and on timber—sufficient duties to keep out the introduction of those articles except from our own colonies. Pretty stout duties therefore, and every man, woman and child in the United Kingdom would at once feel the burden of an increased cost of life and an increased cost of the very means of production. And this added burden is For what purpose? In order to secure that, whereas they have a world-wide trade, they may be able possibly to augment one-fourth of it at the cost of diminishing the three-fourths. I have often wondered at the wisdom of those projectors who recommend to us the capturing of new markets where you are only to spend 20s. and you will get back 10s. when they have such markets at their doors which they might capture if they were Free Traders without guile. I have often wondered at the nonsense of those projectors, but I think their schemes are really more profitable than this scheme of burdening yourself in order to cut down three-fourths of your trade for the possible increase of the other fourth.

My lords and gentlemen, I think perhaps I spend too much time over this. I perhaps do, because the truth is, the proposal has already received its answer. It was no sooner mooted than in the Conference or Congress where it was suggested it was promptly repudiated by the representatives of the greatest Chambers of Commerce in this kingdom. It was no sooner mooted than it was repudiated from the Antipodes. And, indeed, it has been a false dilemma as respects the Antipodes — as respects our Colonies. It is a plan which no Free Trader will take. He does not want it. And no

Protectionist will take it, because he will not gain by it. If your friend is in the bond of iniquity it is no use approaching him with this idle dream. If he is converted, he does not want any more conversion, and the thing as respects ourselves and Australians has been answered already.

But there has come another answer. What has happened in Canada? If there has been one man more than another who has been active in several forms under which this idea has been presented it is Sir Charles Tupper. He has gone up and down the United Kingdom addressing Chambers of Commerce. He has coquetted with Empire Leagues and Fair Trade Leagues, and sent his emissaries to South Africa and Australia. He, perhaps, more than anyone else, inspired the Ottawa Conference. His energy, his ability, his indomitable pluck and industry, we all know and recognise, and the very pivot upon which it turns, the temper and disposition of the great colony, have been manifested this week as utterly hostile to Sir Charles Tupper. You know the result. It was with Canada at his back that he spoke, but Canada is not at his back. He professed to be able to show you the way of uniting an empire together, and his own particular Dominion has turned traitor and will have none of it.

I know it is said that the general election in Canada turned upon other issues. Things always do turn upon other issues. General elections are very complex things. The question of education was mixed up with the question of tariff in Canada, and I am not here to deny that the question of education may be one of the greatest importance in party fortunes. As I say, the question of education was mixed up with the question of tariff in Canada—but in what direction? If you have got a result brought about by two causes, each contributing to that result, you may be at a loss to value exactly the efficiency of each cause in bringing about the result. But if you have two causes operating in different directions, and one prevails, the fact that the other operated in a different direction only shows the strength of that which has prevailed. Education was a very potent factor in the election which happened in Canada this week. Upon whose side did it work? The election turned upon the province of Quebec. In Ontario there was little change, and in Quebec there was a great change. In Quebec the education question was used and employed in the strongest manner by powerful advocates against Mr Laurier, against the Free Trade policy, and therefore as Free Trade has been victorous it is a double victory.

No possible contingency could be more happy than the result of this election in Canada. I think we might be pardoned if we look upon it as a manifest providence that in what was supposed to be the strong-hold of Protection there has uprisen this strong opinion in favour of Free Trade. This last plea for disguised Protection was put before you as a means of uniting the Empire together. But the union of the Empire is as safe with Mr Laurier as with Sir Charles Tupper. The French Canadians are amongst the most attached subjects of the Crown. It has often been said that the last shot which would be fired in America for the British connection would be fired by a French Canadian, and this saying remains as true to-day under Mr Laurier as it was under those who have gone before him. We regard Canada as sealing the fate of this fanciful dream.

I wish I could regard the rest of the continent of America in the same way as I regard Canada. To speak of the United States is a matter of delicacy and difficulty. This much I would say for myself, that I have always been, as I believe myself to be now, a most fervent well-wisher of that great republic, and I remember with satisfaction how in its hours of greatest trial I was associated with my lamented friend, Professor Cairnes, inspired by his teaching, and associated with John Stuart Mill, in wishing for the triumph and union of the great republic. I therefore approach that question with no spirit but that of the purest friendship. But what are we to say? I said something not too laudatory of the statesmanship of our own land in connection with the past. It sometimes seems to me as though the function of a statesman in the United States was not to have a well-considered opinion of his own, but to ascertain as nearly as possible the limits of elasticity of the opinions of other people. In the formation of platforms and the organising of campaigns these are the main objects kept in view. But I remember the M'Kinley tariff brought back a great reaction. The institutions of the republic are such that the national will cannot immediately find expression. The M'Kinley tariff brought about a great reaction, and so I venture to hope—very sanguine may be the expectation—that the M'Kinley presidency will be greater in its effects still. Let the experiment be tried. Let us trust to the good sense of the American people. It is a matter of time, and the promises cannot be at once realised, but I am certain that even from the United States we shall in time get such a response as we have got from Canada, and when this cause, which is the cause of working humanity all over the world, cannot fail of acceptance there.

I have occupied a very long time, but there is one word more I fain would speak before I sit down.

Mr Cobden's statemanship did not end with Free Trade. I know there are many to-day who are ready to indulge in un-generous sneers at the failure of Mr Cob-den's hopes, at the want of realisation of his prophecies, and I daresay those sneers will be echoed in some columns that may be occupied with print on Monday morning. But to those who are disposed to sneer at Mr Cobden, I may recall the language which some of us here remember Mr Dis-

raeli used on Mr Cobden's lamented death,
language of genuine emotion, language of
high appreciation, language of strong admiration, and if it be said that such a tribute
was natural for the time, the place, the circumstances of the hour, I would also remind
those who hear me that the same tribute,
even more freely, more strongly expressed,
is to be found in the conversation of Mr
Disraeli which Mr Matthew Arnold recorded
in his letters, which appeared last winter to
the delight of many readers. Mr Disraeli
appreciated Mr Cobden as a born statesman,
whose ideas are always the ideas of a statesman, broad, generous, vital. Mr Cobden was
a Free Trader, but he looked upon Free
Trade as a means of alleviating the condition of the masses of the workers of the
world, not only directly but indirectly, because he believed that through Free Trade

we could develop the spirit of peace among the nations, and might look forward to the time when war and international jealousy might be little more than the memories of the past. Here, my lords and gentlemen, Mr Cobden's prophecies have been sadly falsified. Within one year of his death there ensued a sharp war between men speaking the same tongue in Central Europe. Within five years there broke out a yet greater war, the effects of which are still too evident among European politics. What does it become us as followers of Mr Cobden to do in the face of such facts as are presented to us in the spectacle of Europe? Aggravated armaments press down the people, envenomed and bitter jealousies exist among the nations. Is it not our part, standing aloof, animated by friendship to all, to show all possible goodwill, in making sacrifice if need be, to bring together those who are thus cruelly apart in being true here, at all events, to the doctrines of the man we honour, in striving to spread the feelings of friendship we entertain by the risks we are prepared to run, the consummation of the hopes upon which he dwelt. Grievous, deplorable as the spectacle of Europe is to-day, it is not viewed by me, at all events, without hope, and in the spirit of Cobden I contemplate it with some hope that the future may redeem the past. Within these last days there has been telegraphed to us, on the highest authority, statements of a *rapprochement* between Italy and France which shows a disposition on the part of the former to throw over the United Kingdom in favour of France. For my part I would say, 'Throw over the United Kingdom if you like, return to the counsels of unity and friendship, be again one with those who were and ought to be your brothers, return again to the attempt to establish freedom and good-will among the nations of Western Europe.'

Nor is this all. Statesmen may hesitate ; statesmen must hesitate. It is the attribute of statesmen to be slow ; perhaps it is their virtue. But those who look below the immediate surface of things, those who try to measure the enduring, the abiding, the growing force of humanity—if you discern as our fathers might have discerned fifty years ago, that the repeal of the Corn Laws was certain, because the movement of the people was in that direction, you may discern the movement among the teeming masses which form the base of society on the continent sentiments of peace and friendship, which may disarm armies and make captains of armies very feeble folk.

I for my part will not choose but cherish this illusion, if illusion it be, but this illusion we can make a certainty if we are bent upon it, if we can only animate our countrymen with the same feeling. Let us as followers of Cobden — let us devote ourselves not to that greed which leads nations to hate one another, to separate themselves in hostile camps, but to those feelings of friendship which should bring them together, and weld the nations of Europe, nay the nations of the world, in bonds of peace.

My lords and gentlemen, it is in this spirit and in the hope that you agree with me therein that I invite you to drink to the Cobden Club.

THE COBDEN CLUB ADDRESS

TO THE

RIGHT HON. CHARLES P. VILLIERS, M.P.

THE COBDEN CLUB ADDRESS TO THE RIGHT HON. CHARLES P. VILLIERS, M.P.

THE Address presented by the Cobden Club on the 26th of June, 1896, the Fiftieth Anniversary of the Repeal of the Corn Laws, in connection with the Cobden Club Corn Law Repeal Commemoration Banquet, to the Right Hon. Charles Pelham Villiers, M.P., the sole survivor of the four Statesmen, Peel, Villiers, Cobden and Bright, to whom the passing of that measure was due ;—

In celebrating triumphs which have become part of our national history, it is an excep-

tional privilege to be able to address congratulations to one who not only played a
leading part in the final contest, but who
led a forlorn hope when the fortress of
prejudice and privilege might well appear
unassailable.   The cause of which you have
been so persevering an advocate—the cause
of all that we know under the name of
Freedom of Trade; the cause of the many
against the few; the cause which asserts the
right of every man to make the best use of
the faculties which God has given him, un-
fettered by iniquitous tributes to his more
powerful neighbours; the cause which achieved
its final triumph in the repeal of the taxes on
food, has, like other great causes, gone through
various stages, and owes its ultimate victory
to a succession of heroic efforts.

The first step was made when philosophers
of the last century proved to the satisfaction

of unprejudiced thinkers that freedom of exchange is an essential condition of successful
production. These philosophers have long
since left us, and all that we can do is to
honour ourselves by honouring their memory.

The next step was made by those who,
in face of the reaction caused by the great
war, of the prejudices of a people influenced
by that reaction, and of the power of a
dominant and victorious oligarchy, presever-
ingly urged upon a hostile and reluctant
legislature the measures which philosophy
had shown to be wise and just.

The third step was to instruct and arouse
the people. This was effected by an agitation, in the Press and on the platform, un-
exampled alike for its moderation and its
power — an agitation which brought home
the truths of the closet to the minds and
consciences of an enlightened people, and,

by its influence on the constituencies, enabled —and even compelled—the great statesmen, of whom one still survives, to bring the long-continued contest to a successful issue.

You, sir, and you alone of living men, have had the privelege of playing a leading part in both these stages. You brought the subject of the Corn Laws before Parliament year after year before the popular agitation commenced. You were associated with the other great men who conducted that agitation; and you had the satisfaction of at last recording your vote in the House of Commons in favour of the cause for which you had so long pleaded. Neither your own constituents nor the people of the country have forgotten what you have done for them. At the present moment, when a general acceptance of the truths taught by you and your colleagues makes this country a triumphant exception — but alas! an exception—to the prejudices of the civilised world; when even in this country those truths are constantly subjected to covert assaults by enemies who dare not profess an open disbelief in them: at such a time your example, and the example of those with whom you acted in the great struggle for Free Trade, may well serve as a warning and encouragement to us, whose duty it is to maintain and hand on to our successors the conquests originally won by you and your colleagues under circumstances of difficulty and discouragement such as we have never experienced.

THOMAS B. POTTER, *Chairman.*
RICHARD GOWING, *Secretary.*

REPLY TO THE COBDEN CLUB'S CORN LAW REPEAL JUBILEE ADDRESS

REPLY TO THE COBDEN CLUB'S CORN LAW REPEAL JUBILEE ADDRESS

BY THE RIGHT HON. CHARLES PELHAM VILLIERS, M.P.

To the Chairman and Committee
of the Cobden Club

GENTLEMEN, — Your courtesy in associating my name with the celebration by the members of the Cobden Club of the fiftieth anniversary of the Repeal of the Corn Laws, and your recognition of the part that I took in the struggle to obtain for our country the inestimable blessings of freedom of trade, are to me a source of sincere gratification, for I cannot but regard your action as an assurance, on the part of your association, of their lively interest in the maintenance of our Free Trade policy, and of their determination, individually and collectively, to exercise 'eternal vigilance' over its preservation unimpared, as the price to be paid for its continued enjoyment in the future; and in this faith I beg to tender you my acknowledgments of the honour you do me in presenting to me your address of congratulation.   The fifty years that have elapsed since the repeal, in furnishing abundant proofs of the wisdom of that policy, constitute as powerful an ally to Free Traders of to-day as was famine, in the words of my good friend Mr Bright, to those of fifty years ago.

Although we are the single nation who have adopted frankly the policy of Free Trade, we must remember that, in introducing his Free Trade Budget on the 27th

January, 1846, Sir Robert Peel expressly declared that he had no guarantee to give that
other nations would follow our example ; and
he made the following memorable statement :—'Wearied with our unavailing efforts
to enter into satisfactory commercial treaties
with other nations, we have resolved at
length to consult our own interests, and not
to punish other countries for the wrong they
do us, in continuing their high duties upon
the importation of our products and manufactures, by continuing high duties ourselves,
encouraging unlawful trade. We have had
no communication with any foreign Government upon the subject of these reductions.'
Then, alluding to the large fiscal reforms
which he had made in the previous five years,
he added, 'It is a fact that other countries
have not followed our example, and have
levied higher duties in some cases upon our

goods. But what has been the result upon the amount of your exports? You have defied the regulations of these countries! Your export trade is greatly increased. Now, Why is that so? Partly because of your acting without wishing to avail your-selves of their assistance; partly because of the smuggler, not engaged by you, in so many continental countries, whom the strict regulations and the triple duties, which are to prevent any ingress of foreign goods, have raised up; and partly, perhaps, because these very precautions against the ingress of your commodities are a burden, and the taxation increasing the cost of production disqualifies the foreigner from competing with you.'

Three years and a half later, on the 6th July, 1849, Sir Robert Peel set forth ex-haustively the facts and reasons which justified the Free Trade policy for which he was responsible, and boldly maintained that the principle of Protection to domestic industry —meaning thereby duties on imports imposed for that purpose and not for revenue —was a vicious principle, and that the best way to compete with hostile tariffs was to encourage free imports. Entirely agreeing with these arguments of Sir Robert Peel, I may perhaps associate myself with them by quoting them:—'So far from thinking the principle of Protection a salutary principle, I maintain that the more widely you extend it the greater the injury you inflict on the national wealth, and the more you cripple the national industry. I found my opinion on these grounds. The capital of the country is the fund from which alone the industry of the country can be maintained. The industry of the country will be promoted

P

in proportion as the capital employed in its maintenance shall be increased. The augmentation of capital must depend upon the saving from annual revenue. If you give for certain articles produced at home a greater price than that for which you can purchase those articles from other countries, there is a proportionate diminution of the saving from annual revenue. If you attempt to redress the injustice which would be done by selecting one particular interest for special protection, if you aver that your object is to extend equal protection to all branches of domestic industry, then I reply that the more extensive that system of Protection the greater will be the loss of aggregate annual revenue, the greater will be the check to the augmentation of capital: that is to say, of the means by which labour is to be maintained. So far from encouraging domestic industry, you are, in the first place, by legislative interference, diverting capital from its natural and most profitable application; and you are, in the second place, by giving more for every article than it is worth, exhausting the source from which alone capital can be maintained and augmented. The principles which should govern the commercial intercourse of nations do not differ from those which regulate the dealings of private individuals. It is the same law which determines the accumulation of wealth by the private trader and the powerful kingdom. We only obscure and mystify the truth by overlooking the principle which governs the dealings of every man of common sense.' Then, admitting that Adam Smith, and J. B. Say and David Hume demonstrated these true principles, Sir R. Peel reminded the House that those principles had been adopted by the merchants and bankers of London, who in 1820 presented a petition—a petition which propounded this doctrine, 'that the maxim of buying in the cheapest market and selling in the dearest, which regulates every merchant in his individual dealings, is strictly applicable as the best rule for the trade of the whole nation,' and declared that it was 'against every restrictive regulation of trade, not essential to the revenue—against all duties merely protective from foreign competition —and against the excess of such duties as are partly for the purpose of revenue and partly for that of Protection,' that the prayer of the petition was respectfully submitted to the wisdom of Parliament.

Such was the admirable expression by Sir Robert Peel of his reasons for repealing the Corn Laws. It remains for us to consider the justification of the policy which has been afforded by fifty years' experience.

If I were asked for proofs that the policy of Free Trade has been justified by its results, I should make answer with one word *' Circumspice !'* For Free Trade has become during the fifty years of our experience a living force of incalculable energy. Of this fact no stronger proof can be urged than the belief in its principles of a succession of eminent Conservative statesmen, including Lord Beaconsfield, Mr W. H. Smith and Lord Randolph Churchill among those who have passed away, as well as the leading members and the great bulk of the Conservative party of the present day; and no one has ever questioned Mr Gladstone's firm adherence to Free Trade since the repeal of the Corn Laws. Nor must we forget Lord Salisbury's expression of opinion that Protection is impossible again in favour of one single interest, and if ever adopted it must be general, but so far as he can see that policy is impossible.

Within the past few months we have seen the present Chancellor of the Exchequer vieing with his predecessor in office in congratulating the nation on its condition of unprecedented prosperity, and each attributing the ability of the nation to bear its great burden of taxation to the soundness of the financial system under which that prosperity has, in the course of fifty years of Free Trade, become the wonder of the civilised world.

Without adventuring upon a lengthy although justifiable review of the abounding proofs of the benefits enjoyed by this country as a result of its adoption of the policy of free importation, it is perhaps

permissible, very briefly, to summarise the
chief results which are so patent that all
may see and verify them.

Taking first the growth of trade, as
evidenced by the increase of our exports
of produce and manufactures, we may compare the total value for the twenty - five
years before the Repeal of the Corn Laws
(1821 to 1845), namely, £1,085,000,000, with
the total value of £3,031,000,000 for the
twenty-five years which followed the Repeal;
an increase of nearly two hundred per cent.!
But even this enormous development of the
export trade during the first twenty-five years
of Free Trade has been exceeded by the
growth during the second period of twenty-
five years, from 1871 to the present year,
the total value of our export trade for these
latter years being £6,299,000,000. But
whereas our export trade has risen so

enormously, in spite of the great and continuous fall of prices during recent years,
our import trade has risen in even greater
proportion, the total value of imports of
merchandise for the years 1871 to 1895
being £9,763,000,000.

By this great foreign trade our people
have benefited in their every day lives, as
may be seen from their largely increased
consumption of articles of food, and by
their being better clothed, better housed,
and better educated.   From the increase of
trade has resulted an extended employment
of the people; and it is matter of common
knowledge that, whereas labour commands a
higher scale of wages than it ever did before,
the working classes are able to obtain more
and better articles, both of necessity and
luxury, from the freedom of importation of
goods from every quarter of the globe.

In view of the excess of our import over
our export trade it has sometimes been contended that we must pay in gold and silver
for this excess of our imports over our exports. How incorrect this contention is may
be seen from the fact that during the years
1870 to 1895 the total excess of our imports
of gold and silver over our exports exceeded
£77,000,000.

Increased comfort for the vast body of the
people has been accompanied by an increase
of thrift on their part; and we learn from
the recent financial statement of the Chancellor of the Exchequer that during the last
ten years the deposits in the savings banks
have more than doubled. Equally satisfactory
is the diminution in the number of paupers.
According to the latest published official return, the number of paupers who were relieved
in England and Wales on the last day of the

quarter ending March 1896 was 739,021, as compared with 897,370 in 1857, although the population has grown in the forty years from 19,000,000 to over 30,000,000. Nowadays the ratio of paupers to inhabitants is about 24 in the thousand, having fallen one-half since 1857, when it was over 47 in the thousand.

The great increase in the wealth of the nation at large is evidenced in many ways, but in none is it more strikingly seen than in the increase of property assessed to the payment of income tax. In 1854 the sum assessed was £287,000,000, and in 1894 the amount was £706,000,000. The decrease in the amount at which land is now assessed as compared with the amount assessed thirty years ago, namely, about £56,000,000 in 1894, and £62,000,000 in 1865, is insignificant when compared with the *rise* in the amount assessed upon house property, namely, from £68,000,000 in 1865 to £149,000,000 in 1894.

Perhaps. however, as satisfactory a proof of the continuous prosperity of the country as any is furnished by the rapid rate at which the National Debt is being paid off, largely out of the successive surpluses of annual revenue over expenditure. In 1856, after the Crimean War, the Debt stood at £829,000,000, or about £29, 12s. per head of the population. In 1895 it had been reduced to £660,000,000, or about £17, 6s. per head of the population; and the Chancellor of the Exchequer told us that the amount at which it stood on 31st March 1896 was £652,000,000. In the last thirteen years we have paid off £100,000,000.

In face of such facts as these, substantiated as they are by figures taken from the official records, who can venture to dispute that the country has benefited, and continues to benefit,

under the fiscal system known as Free Trade,
which few would *now* deny to be 'just, wise,
and beneficial?'

The wisdom of the principles enunciated
by the philosophers of the last century, and
fought for by their disciples in the first half
of the present, has been demonstrated in the
fullest measure by the immense increase of
material prosperity, and its accompanying
moral welfare, of the last fifty years, of
which the facts and figures that I have given
are the complete confirmation.

You can now contrast the fifty years that
have passed since the Repeal of the Corn
Laws with the thirty years during which
they were in operation. In the earlier period
there was constant distress in the country,
often accompanied by incendiary outbreaks.
Time after time Parliamentary inquiry was
made into the causes of the distress which

pressed so hardly upon both the agricultural classes and the operatives of the towns. Prices of wheat fluctuated from 53s. in January 1816 to 112s. in June 1817, and by the following September had fallen to 74s. a quarter! The Select Committee of 1821 reported that the agricultural distress of 1820 was, like other similar instances, largely consequent upon abundant harvests in the United Kingdom in the two previous years. Year after year the Government of the country had to face a diminishing revenue, until the oppressive tariff began gradually to be reduced. Very slowly the condition of the people then improved; until, under the beneficial operation of a tariff granting free importation, prosperity at last advanced 'by leaps and bounds.'

To you, gentlemen, and to those who share your convictions, it remains as a sacred duty to secure that the millions of electors in this country are not seduced in the future from their allegiance to Free Trade, which would assuredly result in a condition more disastrous to our multiplied millions than even was experienced in the evil days of the supremacy of Protection. Of such a result I have no fear; and in the words of Sir Robert Peel, I say, 'It is my consolation that *never* will such a Corn Law be re-enacted in England.' —I am, gentlemen, yours faithfully,

C. P. VILLIERS.

ADDITIONS TO MR VILLIERS'S REPLY

The following are appendices enclosed by the Right Honourable Charles P. Villiers with the above reply :—

SIR ROBERT PEEL IN 1849

In the speech of 6th July 1849, in reply

to Mr Disraeli, Sir Robert Peel set forth exhaustively the facts and reasons which justified the Free Trade policy for which he was responsible :—

'In bringing forward the present motion, the hon. gentleman, the Member for Buckinghamshire, observed, speaking of our recent legislation, "That we have established a new commercial system, which mistakes the principles upon which a profitable exchange can take place between nations ; that we can only encounter the hostile tariffs of foreign countries by countervailing duties ; that such a system occasions not scarcity and dearness, but abundance and cheapness."

'Now, in opposition to these doctrines, I boldly maintain that the principle of Protection to domestic industry, meaning thereby legislative encouragement for the purpose of Protection, duties on imports imposed for that purpose and not for revenue, is a vicious principle. I contest the hon. gentleman's assumption that you cannot fight hostile tariffs by free imports. I so totally dissent from that assumption that I maintain that the best way to compete with hostile tariffs is to encourage Free Imports. So far from thinking the principle of Protection a salutary principle, I maintain that the more widely you extend it, the greater the injury you inflict on the national wealth, and the more you cripple the national industry.

'I found my opinion on these grounds. The capital of the country is the fund from which alone the industry of the country can be maintained. The industry of the country will be promoted in proportion as the capital employed in its maintenance shall be increased. The augmentation of capital must depend upon the saving from annual revenue. If you give for certain articles produced at home a greater price than that for which you can purchase those articles from other countries, there is a proportionate diminution of the saving from annual revenue. If you attempt to redress the injustice which would be done by selecting one particular interest for special protection, if you aver that your object is to extend equal protection to all branches of domestic industry, then I reply, that the more extensive that system of Protection, the greater will be the aggregate loss of annual revenue, the greater will be the check to the augmentation of capital; that is to say, of the means by which labour is to be maintained. So far from encouraging domestic industry, you are, in the first place, by legislative interference, diverting capital from its natural and most profitable application; and you are, in the second place, by giving more for every

Q

article than it is worth, exhausting the source from which alone capital can be maintained and augmented. . . . The principles which should govern the commercial intercourse of nations do not differ from those which regulate the dealings of private individuals. . . . It is the same law which determines the accumulation of wealth by the private trader and the powerful kingdom. . . .

'No doubt it would be for the advantage of trade—for our own advantage and for the advantage of the countries with which we deal—that hostile tariffs should be reduced. Unquestionable as would be the benefit derived from their reduction, still, if that benefit cannot be obtained, I contend that by the attempt at retaliation you would aggravate your own loss. Let this also be borne in mind, that the retaliatory system, after it has once been abandoned, is infinitely more diffi-

cult than the continued adherence to it might
have been. To re-establish duties upon the
import of foreign produce, to be regulated by
the principle of Reciprocity, would be accompanied with insuperable difficulties. You have
no alternative but to maintain that degree of
Free Trade which you have established, and
gradually to extend it so far as considerations
of revenue will permit.'

FACTS RELATING TO FIFTY YEARS OF FREE TRADE

I. That the value of our Export Trade
   rose rapidly after the Repeal of the
   Corn Laws and the introduction of
   Free Trade.

II. That the value of our Import Trade
    rose even more rapidly after 1846
    than did our Export Trade.

III. That under the operation of the Free Trade tariff we have imported a far larger amount of gold and silver than we have exported.

IV. That the general wealth of the nation has immensely increased, as is proved by the growth of property assessable to the Income Tax.

V. That the savings of the people have increased enormously.

VI. That pauperism has diminished by one-half in the last forty years.

VII. That the consumption of food has greatly increased per head of the population.

VIII. That this nation is the best fed nation in the world, though the country produces the smallest amount of food stuffs.

IX. That the National Debt has been diminished by £177,000,000 in the last forty years.

IMPORTS AND EXPORTS

Total Value of British and Irish Produce and Manufactures Exported from the United Kingdom in the Quarters ending 31st March :—

	1894.	1895.	1896.
To British Possessions	£19,702,028	£16,774,994	£21,021,723
To Foreign Countries......	£34,228,204	£35,945,367	£40,211,320

Total Value of Merchandise Imported into the United Kingdom in the Quarters ending 31st March :—

	1894.	1895.	1896.
From British Possessions	£24,454,191	£23,571,576	£23,520,598
From Foreign Countries	£83,260,484	£77,115,428	£88,698,312

Total Value of the Trade in the Quarters ending 31st March between the United Kingdom and

	1894.	1895.	1896.
British Possessions.........	£44,156,219	£40,346,570	£44,542,321
Foreign Countries..........	£117,488,688	£113,060,795	£128,909,632

For the First Three Months of 1896 the
Total Imports of Gold and Silver   £11,640,818
„   Exports   „   „   9,634,334
Balance of Imports over Exports = £2,006,484

THE END

www.ingramcontent.com/pod-product-compliance
Lightning Source LLC
Chambersburg PA
CBHW020853270326
41928CB00006B/681